# WAGES<sup>TO</sup>
# &lt;WEALTH&gt;

## 11 Steps to turn your wages
## into the life you want to live.

David H. Nolan
www.davidhnolan.com

FIRST EDITION

This publication is designed to provide accurate and authoritative information
in regard to the subject matter covered. It is sold with the understanding that
the author is not engaged in rendering legal, accounting or other professional
service. If legal advice or other expert assistance is required, the services of a
competent professional person should be sought.

-from a Declaration of Principles jointly adopted by a Committee of the
American Bar Association and a Committee of Publishers

## ACKNOWLEDGEMENTS

The author would like to acknowledge the assistance received from Helene
Kempe in her invaluable assistance in the production of this book. Her
patience and ongoing support are greatly appreciated.

# TABLE OF CONTENTS

# CHAPTER 1

# ALWAYS PAY YOURSELF FIRST

Lesson number one is to pay yourself first before you pay anyone else. Why? Because it is you that expends all the energy to earn the income that you earn and it is your right to be paid for the work you do. If you go to work for an employer then you rightly expect that employer to pay you for your labours. To pay you money so that you can enjoy your life by using the money you earn to purchase the things in life that you deem to be of importance to you. Therefore, it stands to reason that if we expect our employers to pay us for our labour, then we should also pay ourselves. In order to achieve financial success we must be more important to ourselves than we are to others.

I know this may sound a little odd at first but here's what you need to do to create any form of wealth in your life. Pay yourself FIRST each and every time you receive income from any source. There are no exceptions to this golden rule. You may remember that once upon a time our parents and grandparents called this saving, and so should we. But it is not saving as your parents or grandparents might have imagined. It is not saving by putting money under the mattress or in a tin box in a cupboard. It is saving with a purpose, and that purpose is to create wealth. Saving has always been seen as a way to amass money to purchase the things we want and desire without going into debt to buy them. The saving I am referring to here is not for purchasing goods and services, it is to build YOUR wealth. Naturally you would save for the things in life you want, rather than go into debt for them. Savings for goods and services should be kept in a separate account from your wealth creation savings.

Building YOUR wealth starts with you paying yourself first each and every time you receive income from any source and by doing so you are actually creating an investment account that you will, in time employ in carefully chosen, safe investments to create more money to add to your investment account. Through creating this habit of paying yourself first and keeping the money you save for investment purposes you will become wealthier, GUARANTEED! You see, wealth is created by amassing money to be used for investment purposes and for the acquisition of valuable, tradable assets such as your home, shares in public companies and government bonds. These assets that you purchase with money saved in your wealth account will become your financial provider in your retirement years and will also become part of your legacy for your family in future years. A legacy that if continued to be built on by your family will become very large no matter how little you put away each week. True wealth is built over time and the longer the savings are made the greater the financial rewards.

Starting the process is the hardest part because many of us believe that we can barely get from pay cheque to pay cheque let alone take some of it away. If we reduce our disposable income how on earth will we survive? There is always too much month at the end of the money, so to speak. It is difficult enough to make ends meet with what we have without having to survive on less. However, I can assure you that many people have been in exactly this situation and had the same belief that you might have that it would be impossible to survive on less money, but they do and they have. Just look around you at people you know who have been faced with a financial crisis perhaps a lost job or an emergency bill to pay. Did they survive? Of course they did, it might not have been pleasant, but they survived. Not only did they manage to change their habits to accommodate their lower disposable income, they have also got a new feeling, a feeling of achievement because they have conquered their financial challenge, possibly for the first time in their lives. Imagine what your friends would have been able to do if they had paid themselves first from their very first pay cheque. They would have had money to pay their way and perhaps not have had to suffer the financial hardships they might have suffered. Are you in the same position? Is it you who has had the financial challenges all your life?

>

**As you monitor your increase in net worth you will find an amazing thing happens.**

Consider for a moment that each week you go to work and earn your wages or you are self employed and you run your business and get money in for your labours, by what amount have you increased your personal net worth? By this I mean, how much richer, financially are you week after week? You see to get rich or achieve financial independence you need to make a habit out of getting rich and one way you can do this is to track your net worth each week, or month. As you monitor your increase in net worth you will find an amazing thing happens. You will find that it gets easier to create wealth as you see that you are actually succeeding. By paying yourself first, each and every pay day, you can actually watch your net worth, your personal wealth increase in real time. This is not magic, this is FACT! Close your eyes for a moment and imagine looking at your bank account balance each pay day and seeing it get higher and higher. Isn't that a great feeling? Doesn't it look good, your name on your account and getting larger and larger week by week? You are getting richer and richer week by week. You see, if you can imagine this, then you can DO IT! One of the great skills employed by successful people the world over is their ability to imagine things they want them to be. So start imagining your bank

To start your new wealth building process I recommend that you place 10% of all your net income into an account for YOU. That's right 10% of all you earn should be put aside for your personal future wealth. *"What's that? 10% of my income, are you mad?"* I hear you say. No, I am not mad in fact 10% is the minimum you should put away each and every time you get paid. Think about it for a minute. All I am really asking you to do is to pay yourself 10% of your net income as reward for giving up a part of your life, and a vital part of your life at that. Whilst we are young and fit we are able to sell our labour for money, we call it work, so why wouldn't we want to place at least a 10% of our net income as minimum reward for this? Imagine if you earn $500.00 per week net income, all I am saying is that you should put away $50.00! Are you not worth $50.00? If you are not paying yourself first, you have given up another week of your life and still failed to provide for your own retirement. So why do we struggle to pay ourselves a mere 10% which is really such a pittance.

After all, do we not work so that we can retire? If we could retire earlier we would, the main reason we don't is because we don't have enough...what? MONEY! If you learn to live on a little less for a little while you will be able to retire earlier and have more money to enjoy your retirement years with.

**The more you save for yourself the greater your wealth will become.**

Living on 10% less income may appear difficult at first, and in many cases it may need a change of life habits. However, ask yourself this question, how much have I amassed in personal wealth during my working life? Have I amassed more than 10% of all that I have earned? If the answer is yes then well done, you are in the minority of working people. If the answer is no then you should not be happy with your answer and you need to change what you are doing. I would suggest that you are not happy with your current situation BECAUSE you have not been paying yourself for all your hard work. You have not been focussed on creating your own wealth. You are letting your retirement slip away from you. Once you start to follow this golden rule you will begin to see that you are getting richer each and every pay day.

In fact, this action is so powerful that you will even want to add more to your self-pay as often as you can. Paying yourself 10% of all you earn is only the starting point. The objective is to increase your self-pay to the highest level you can whilst maintaining the lifestyle you choose to live today. If you can afford to save at a rate greater than 10% of your earnings, say 15% or even 20% or more then do so. The more you save for yourself the greater your wealth will become.

Let's look at a couple of examples with some real dollar amounts to see just how powerful this process of self payment can be. Let's imagine that you are earning $400.00, $500.00 or $700.00 per week net and you are now going to pay yourself 10% per week. As the weeks progress you will see the following amounts increase in your bank account.

| PERIOD | AMOUNT SAVED PER WEEK | | |
|---|---|---|---|
| | $40.00 | $50.00 | $70.00 |
| At the end of week 1 | $40.00 | $50.00 | $70.00 |
| At the end of week 2 | $80.00 | $100.00 | $140.00 |
| At the end of week 10 | $400.00 | $500.00 | $700.00 |
| At the end of week 20 | $800.00 | $1,000.00 | $1,400.00 |
| At the end of week 30 | $1,200.00 | $1,500.00 | $2,100.00 |
| At the end of week 40 | $1,600.00 | $2,000.00 | $2,800.00 |
| At the end of the 1st year | $2,080.00 | $2,600.00 | $3,640.00 |
| At the end of the 2nd year | $4,160.00 | $5,200.00 | $7,280.00 |
| At the end of the 3rd year | $6,240.00 | $7,800.00 | $10,920.00 |
| At the end of the 4th year | $8,320.00 | $10,400.00 | $14,560.00 |
| At the end of the 5th year | $10,400.00 | $13,000.00 | $18,200.00 |
| At the end of the 10th year | $20,800.00 | $26,000.00 | $36,400.00 |

Now let's look at an example with saving 15% of your income. Let's imagine the same earnings $400.00, $500.00 or $700.00 per week net and you are now going to pay yourself 15% per week and as the weeks progress you will see the following amounts in your bank account.

| PERIOD | AMOUNT SAVED PER WEEK | | |
|---|---|---|---|
| | $60.00 | $75.00 | 105.00 |
| At the end of week 1 | $60.00 | $75.00 | 105.00 |
| At the end of week 2 | $120.00 | $150.00 | $210.00 |
| At the end of week 10 | $600.00 | $750.00 | $1,050.00 |
| At the end of week 20 | $1,200.00 | $1,500.00 | $2,100.00 |
| At the end of week 30 | $1,800.00 | $2,250.00 | $3,150.00 |
| At the end of week 40 | $2,400.00 | $3,000.00 | $4,200.00 |
| At the end of the 1st year | $3,120.00 | $3,900.00 | $5,460.00 |
| At the end of the 2nd year | $6,240.00 | $7,800.00 | $10,920.00 |
| At the end of the 3rd year | $9,360.00 | $11,700.00 | $16,380.00 |
| At the end of the 4th year | $12,480.00 | $15,600.00 | $21,840.00 |
| At the end of the 5th year | $15,600.00 | $19,500.00 | $27,300.00 |
| At the end of the 10th year | $31,200.00 | $39,000.00 | $54,600.00 |

And so on.

As you can see, even without adding any earnings from interest you are, by paying yourself 10% or even 15% per week, creating a real net worth that will benefit you into your retirement years and beyond. And as the years go by you will be earning interest which will make your nest egg grow even faster, but more on that later. For now all you need to understand is that by making an effort to pay yourself every week you are on the road to financial independence.

These are very simple examples and deliberately so. I do not wish to confuse the issue with regards to interest rates, inflation, increases in wages etc. All I want you to see here is that with a committed effort to pay yourself first you can in fact, over time, make a difference to your net worth. You will be on the road to creating wealth for yourself, possibly for the first time in your life. This journey will give you enormous pleasure and great satisfaction as you watch your nest egg grow. Pleasure in knowing that you can do it and that you can help others in your life who struggle with money to do it also, by leading the way for them to follow you. It is quite amazing once people see that it is not magic, and that creating wealth is a simple process which once started gains momentum over time and just gets easier and easier. In fact, the journey of a thousand miles starts with the first step and so it is with investing and creating wealth. In order to amass thousands of dollars you first of all need to save the first dollar, then the second dollar and so on. It is impossible to get too even $100.00 if you don't save the first dollar. And yet, many people when asked what they want in life will say financial independence and still do not understand that you have to save your dollars effectively one at a time. Simply try and count to 100 without counting every single number...you can't, whenever you stop at a number and don't include the next one you fail. Try it, 1,2,3,4,5,6,....see, if I don't add 7 I can't get to 8 and beyond. This is exactly how savings works. You start with $1, then $2, then $3 and so on. You amass wealth one step at a time, one dollar at a time.

Now I can hear you say, "*it would take too long if all I could do was save $1 at a time*", and you are absolutely right. We save in multiples of $1 based on our ability to earn money and our even greater ability to save it! If you earn money in hundreds of dollars you will probably start saving in tens of dollars. If you earn money in thousands of dollars you should be saving in hundreds, if not thousands of dollars on a regular basis. The amount you save should reflected the amount you earn. The best way to do this is to save a minimum fixed percentage of your income each and every pay day. This way, whatever you earn will have a direct correlation to your savings and vice versa. If you truly want to master this wealth creation process all you need to do is save the highest percentage of your income you can. If you can get to a point where your savings are the highest part of your total monthly expenditure then you truly are on the right path. A path to financial independence where your future life is yours to control debt free and with the financial ability to explore all those wonderful things you dream of. When you apply the principles in this lesson with the other lessons in wealth creation you will be well on your way to financial independence.

> **If you can get to a point where your savings are the highest part of your total monthly expenditure then you truly are on the right path.**

However, as with all things there has to be a starting point and in creating wealth lesson one, paying you FIRST is the only real starting point that has been proven to work over generations. So go on, start today and put aside a minimum of 10% of your income for YOU, after all YOU deserve to be paid for your efforts, don't you? Because if you don't then who does? But, I hear you say once again, "I can't afford to live on what I earn, how can I save 10% of my income"? So I am going to show you how to do just that. In Chapter Two I am going to show you how to get control of your money and start paying yourself first. It is not rocket science but it does take a little discipline and once you have the discipline you will be amazed at just how easy it really can be for you to save 10% of your income for yourself.

# CONTROL
# WHAT YOU SPEND

This is the second lesson - control what you spend. It sounds obvious to control what you spend doesn't it? Yet, it is amazing how many people live beyond their financial means. They spend more each week or month than they earn and are going backwards financially. Not only that, they are in fact committing their future earning ability to today's living. They are committing themselves to have to work tomorrow for the living they have done today. This is not how to create wealth and it certainly is not fair to you to put yourself into a situation where you have to work to pay for past indulgences. What happens if you lose your ability to earn money, either temporarily or more permanently? What will you do then? Get into more debt? Call on your family and friends to look after you?

Controlling what you spend is paramount to wealth creation in as much as if you live within your means today you will create a better lifestyle for yourself in the future by amassing wealth. How many times have you looked at wealthy people and wished you had their lifestyle? How many times have you wished that you could pay the bills without stressing or worrying where the money was going to come from? The concept of living within your means is not only logical it is empowering. Living within your means by controlling what you spend will keep you out of debt. Debt is that evil little thing that commits your future earning potential to today's life style. Imagine living debt free. How good would it be to have all that extra money to do things with instead of paying interest to someone because you wanted to live ahead of your time. Imagine getting to keep all the money you earned instead of having to pay your creditors first and then live off what's left over. How much more power would you have as an individual? How good would it feel to say I can afford this or that without using credit? This power is yours to take, but first there needs to be some pain. Just like going to the gym for the first few times. As you learn to work your unused muscles they ache a little and then they get used to it and don't hurt anymore. The same process occurs when you take control of your finances for the first time, or perhaps regain control after a period of time without control. A little bit of pain or in this case discomfort for a long term gain. If you can't afford something learn to admit it and save for it. This is muscle control of the highest order, this is controlling your mental processes and your emotional mood swings. This is the pain part!

Living in the real world requires real understanding of what you can and cannot afford...today! By living within your means you are giving yourself the best chance to create wealth where the lifestyle of your future can be whatever you choose it to be. It is no secret that people who live within their means tend to be wealthier, happier and less stressed about money. Not because they work harder than you or I might or that they are any smarter than you or I. They just

>

**The concept of living within your means is not only logical it is empowering.**

understand that living within their means today means they can improve how they live in the future and so can you and I if we do the same things they do. The future is yours to control financially and it is up to you to plan and live the future you plan. If you live beyond your means today and don't change your excessive spending habit it means you will always be living beyond your means until such time as you can't cope anymore and things go all wrong.

If you don't use parts of your body on a regular basis they become weak and in some cases suffer atrophy to the point where they no longer function at all. Your money habits do the same thing. By exercising your saving habit you suppress your spending habit and that is a good thing. If the spending habit gets out of control then we are in for a tough ride. It is like eating the wrong food; if we do, we get fat and suffer all kinds of ailments as a consequence. But, if we eat the right food our body flourishes and we thrive, living longer, healthier and happier. Good money health is vital to your quality of life because without it you could be in for a rocky ride.

What can go wrong? I would suggest practically anything and everything in your life that has meaning to you. There is more than enough physical and anecdotal evidence of the suffering people have endured when they are lacking money. Families fall apart, stress levels increase and cause illness and even suicides occur, all because of money! I don't wish to sound like a doomsayer, but these things happen and they can all be avoided. Money is a system of barter for society to use to trade amongst ourselves, it is not the be all and end all of living, yet we place so much emphasis on money that we allow it to affect our lives to the point where some people have committed suicide as a result of money problems. Many, if not all of these problems can be avoided completely if you learn to live within your means.

> **You take control and possession of your future and that of your family, rather than have your creditors control how long you work and to some degree the quality of life you can expect to live.**

Living within your means by controlling what you spend your money on makes sense. As long as you practice this good habit you will find that money becomes your friend not your enemy. Instead of committing your future working life to paying off debt because you spent too much money, by reducing your expenditure and paying yourself first you will create a situation where your future commitment to working actual reduces not increases. You take control and possession of your future and that of your family, rather than have your creditors control how long you work and to some degree the quality of life you can expect to live. Surely, as we age we should get to have a say in how we live our lives. It is understandable a young person that our naivety lets us do things that are not in our own best interests but as we age we should be learning how to control our actions emotions and finances. I am not talking about becoming an investment guru and having degrees in economics or high finance. I am talking about a simple strategy of paying yourself 10% of everything you earn and saving this money for your future. You don't need to understand high finance to do this, you simply need to take control over your own spending habits...and anyone can do that!

So where do you start to control what you spend? You may have been living in denial or ignorance of your actual living costs and as such debt, primarily credit card debt is getting a tight grip on you and your future earnings. The way to remove that vice like grip is for you to set a budget and stick to it. *"Oh no, not a budget, I can't work to a budget, I earn my money and I deserve to spend it any way I like and no one is giving me a budget!"* I hear you plead. Alas this is true, however, you may not realise this but if you have debts that you are paying off, such as credit card, then the credit

> Go on, stop and dream for a few minutes
> - I dare you.
> Imagine not having any debts to pay.

card provider is in fact setting your budget for you. They are telling you, with the full force of the law to pay them a part of every dollar you earn until such time as the debt is repaid. They are controlling a portion of your present and future disposable income before you have a chance the spend it! Talk about not having a budget. You go out and earn your income as we all do and you then have to put aside a portion of that income to pay the debts. Who's in control of your money here? Who is setting the budget, you or the credit card company or other creditor? If it is your money shouldn't you determine how it is spent, shouldn't you develop the budget? Take control back for yourself and stop letting the creditors control you.

To take back control you need to adopt a budget that YOU set that will apply to you. Doing this will give you the power and control to get rid of debts and have access to ALL of your net income not just the part that's left after you pay the debts. Imagine how good that would feel to be debt free. Go on, stop and dream for a few minutes - I dare you. Imagine not having any debts to pay. Imagine living in a home where there is no mortgage, no credit card debt no auto finance, imagine. Feels good doesn't it? Well that feeling can be yours to keep with a little effort on your part and a plan of attack that will work. The plan is what we call a budget. A plan that will clearly show in time and value when you will be debt free and just how much money you will have at your disposal. Money you can employ to help you stop working sooner, or at least to control the future quality of your life. The time it takes is immaterial to the point that it takes as long as it takes, but to not make any effort because you think it will take too long simply means that you are admitting that you are happy to live in debt for ever. Is this true? Are you happy to live in debt for ever and not have control of your own money ever again? It doesn't sound too good to me, but hey, it's your life, your money and your choice. A simple budget is all that is needed to get you started and you can do it in just a few minutes.

Writing a budget requires you to have a good long hard look at where your money is going. Is your hard earned money going into a wealth creation plan and a plan for retirement, or is it going into a few short term luxuries and treats or even worse is it being wasted on stuff you don't even need?

> **Writing a budget requires you to have a good long hard look at where your money is going.**

Let's look at an example of stuff you don't need that if avoided will save you money and could even have other benefits as well. Let's look at take away or junk food. The amount of money people spend on take away or junk food is staggering, and why? Is it so hard to pack a meal if you go out for the day? Is it so hard to eat a meal earlier or later if you are going to be away from home at meal time? Is it so hard to prepare food that is nourishing and economical? Spending your hard earned money on junk food is crazy. Imagine this, if you earn income at a rate of $15.00 per hour. Or $600.00 per week before tax and your tax was 30% of your income you would earn approximately $400.00 per week, net to take home. That's equivalent to $10.00 per hour. So you rock up to the junk food shop and you buy a basic meal and a can of drink and voila you have spent $10.00 or more. Here's my question, imagine that you had no money in your pocket and you are walking down the street. You start to feel a little hungry and decide to eat at a junk food shop, would you volunteer to work for one whole hour for a basic meal and can of soft drink? Would you go into the shop and trade one hour of your labour for that simple meal? I doubt too many of us would, especially if we are not starving to death but merely being lazy or overly indulgent. Whatever it is just think about it next time you are out and want to buy junk food. How much time do you have to work to pay for that meal? This is how change occurs we look at things differently for the first time.

income – expenses = NET INCOME

Let's look at your spending in a different way than you might be used to. A way that can and will empower you to change your life today and into the future. The first thing you must do is identify exactly how much you get to keep in your pocket for each hour of your life you give up to go to work. To do this all you need to do is to take the amount of money you take home each pay day. Then subtract from that the amount of money you pay each week or fortnight to pay your debts, other than rent. Then divide what's left by the number of hours you had to work to get that income.

This is your REAL net hourly income based on the lifestyle choices you have made thus far in your life. By taking out the debts you are paying for past lifestyle choices and therefore that money is not available for present and future lifestyle choices. Let's look at some figures as an example. Let's assume that you bring home $550.00 per week and you pay a credit card of $120.00 per month, or for the sake of simplicity, $30.00 per week. You also pay other small debts of about $20.00 per week, maybe a store card or a personal loan. That's a total of $50.00 per week for debts. This means that your actual disposable income to pay for all your living expenses is actually $550.00 minus $50.00 for debt payments leaving $500.00 per week for living expenses. If you work a 38 hour week as many Australians do then your net disposable hourly rate is $500.00 divided by 38 equals $13.15 per hour approximately. So for every $13.15 you spend you have to work for one hour.

Imagine what happens then if you go spending on credit cards or other store credit for items that you really could live without. Let's imagine that you want to buy the latest LCD big screen television you have just seen in the store. Wow, it is a bargain it is only $1,650.00 and has a huge saving of $600.00 off! Consider this, if you buy this item on credit over three years at say $60.00 per month with interest added. What you are in fact doing is committing yourself to working 4.56 hours per month ($60.00/$13.15) just to own this television!

**Placing a high value on your labour will assist you in sticking to a planned budget.**

That's 4.56 hours per month for three years, or if you like a total of 164.16 hours (4.56x36 months) of future work on your part. Do you like television that much? Are there cheaper alternatives? Of course there are.

Now I'm not saying you shouldn't buy the television. What I am saying, is that you should consider if working 4.56 hours per month is worth it. Especially given that the television will depreciate as it gets older and becomes less valuable. Reading and studying instead of watching television will make you more knowledgeable and knowledge can be converted into more income. Watching television hour after hour is meaningless and will, in this instance only keep you locked into debt. Is this a tough choice? I don't think so, do you? By thinking in terms of hours worked rather than meaningless numbers you will empower yourself to learn to live within your means and cherish your time and its true financial value to you.

By valuing your spending based on the number of hours you have to work in order to have the money to spend you are in fact looking at money in a different light. Economists will tell you that as you commence work in your younger years you will trade your labour for money. As you age you will need to use money to earn money because you will lose your ability to perform labour. If you are relying on your ability to provide labour into your older years you are heading for a disappointment. As you rightly know, as we all age we lose our ability to remain fit and agile, especially compared to when we were younger. And let's face it, who wants to be performing manual labour when we should be comfortably retired. Placing a high value on your labour will assist you in sticking to a planned budget. It will empower you to stop over committing your future earning capability. The less you commit your future earnings the more of them you will get to keep for YOU!

A well written budget will provide you with a guiding light to your financial freedom. To start what I suggest you do is identify all of your expenses each month and write them down on a piece of paper or on a spreadsheet if you are computer literate and have access to a computer. Do this with actual expenses not made up ones. Have a look at the actual bills you pay and use those true amounts, do not make them up unless you do not have exact figures on hand. Once you have done this you can then enter your income each pay cycle as a total. The difference between your expenses and your income is your net weekly position. If you are in positive mode then you will be able to save this money for investment or for future purchases, as our parents and grandparents used to. If however you have a  negative in your total then you clearly have a problem. You are living beyond your means and this will eventually catch up with you. You are committing your future working ability for living today. What do you think the future will hold for you? Remember as you age your body slows down and your ability to earn money diminishes.

One good idea I recommend to use to manage money is to use a simple daily calendar displayed in a prominent position in your home, perhaps on the fridge for example. You can get these from many sources for free, try your local businesses. Each day you and your family write on the calendar any money you or they spend during the day. Write the amount and the item on the calendar as you spend your money and have your family do the same then at the end of the month total up all the daily expenditures and write this on a list showing the amount and the purchase. What you will see will be quite startling. How much money gets waisted on things we really could live without or we could have bought at a lower cost alternative. Remember that for every dollar we over spend we are giving up our valuable labour to do so. Labour that takes its toll regardless of your profession we all get older and less physically capable.

Close scrutiny like this is needed if you are not necessarily a good money manager and will as a result empower you to start controlling your financial future. Controlling your financial future is what you are looking to do, so these simple little tools will get you up and running and start to give you back control of your money and of your valuable time. Time spent working

> **Managing money can have a profound effect on how you get to spend your 60 seconds per minute.**

to pay others due to our own lack of control of our spending habits is a waste. The one thing that we all have as humans, irrespective of our financial wealth is we all get 60 seconds in every minute of every day. Be you the president of the most powerful country on earth or a babe in arms, sixty seconds per minute is all you get and what you do with it is entirely up to you. Managing money can have a profound effect on how you get to spend your 60 seconds per minute. Not just the present 60 seconds but the future sixty second minutes that lie ahead.

Now that you understand that paying yourself first and managing your monthly budget will put you on the road to wealth creation you will want to start those saved up dollars to work for you. By learning how to put your money to work for you instead of you working for it is the third step in the road to wealth creation and in Chapter Three we look at just how you can do that. As you learn to put your money to work you will discover new ways to use money and to save money, all of which will add to your nest egg.

CHAPTER 3

# MAKE YOUR MONEY MULTIPLY

As you embark on changing your financial situation and have started paying yourself first and taken control of your money, your next step is to make your money multiply. In other words you can start investing your money to earn more money. Just as you go to work for your money you can employ your money to earn money for you. Making your money work for you is one of the economic theories that we all need to follow. Remember when we are young we trade our labour for money and as we get older we need to have our money earn money to free up our labour. The earlier you start learning how to put your money to work the better. Like all things in life putting money to work and work effectively is a learned skill and is not something that just happens. You need to learn how to employ money for its optimum return and the sooner you start the better. Many people fail to start their basic wealth creation plan of paying themselves first because they do not understand investing. They make this excuse because they think that you need to understand investing to make any money. This is clearly not true. In fact some of the world's smartest people when it comes to money actually work for other people and can help you make money too. One name that comes to mind is the world famous investor Mr Warren Buffet. There are thousands of investors big and small who make money from hiring the very capable skills of Mr Buffet. By investing in companies that Mr Buffet manages, they are by default earning money from his personal skills and labour. Accessing Mr Buffet may not be available for us all so there needs to be alternatives and there are.

One way you can put your money to work is to hire the services of a professional financial adviser. I am talking about a person who has the demonstrable skills, knowledge, and proper authority to assist in putting your money to work. These people are experienced in many types of investment products and will be able to advise you on how to use your money to generate income and or capital growth. They will effectively put your money to work for you. Using a licensed financial planner will give you the support and a solid base of knowledge for you to start learning how to manage your money in the most effective way. Licensed financial planners are trained professionals who work for fees to help people like you and me to put our money to work. They are well versed in all forms of investment types and can be relied upon to assist you, even if you have no investment knowledge whatsoever. A professional financial adviser will guide you on your wealth creation journey and as you go along will inevitably teach you what investments are all about. You do not necessarily need to learn at all, but it would be wise to learn as much as you can to be able to make informed investment decisions for yourself. If you do not have any desire to learn then you should be able to rely on a professional financial adviser to do the job for you.

> **One way you can put your money to work is to hire the services of a professional financial adviser.**

Should you elect not to use a financial adviser and instead, elect to manage your own money, there are many ways for you to learn what to do. One way is to use the internet as a resource guide for investment knowledge. The internet is full of amazing information about thousands of subjects but not too many would be as exhaustive as *investing*. There are literally tens of thousands of pages of information just waiting for you to read. Pages range from basic savings plans and investments to highly complex investment strategies. All online and mostly available free of charge. All you need to do is log on and start reading, asking questions and exploring the world of investments.

> Another way to learn about investing is to source some of the many thousands of books available on investing money.

Another way to learn about investing is to source some of the many thousands of books on investing money. There are investment books available at all leading book stores and in public libraries. Once again they cover the full gambit of investment knowledge from investing for absolute beginners to highly specialised investment strategies. In fact this book is one of the many available to help you get started. Whatever source you use to gain knowledge and to learn new skill be sure to give due consideration to the motivation of the author of the work you are learning from. For example, books and web sites promoting property investments are usually written by people in the property investment field and tend to have a bias towards property investing. Whereas investment books and web sites promoting share investments or any of their derivatives are usually written by people who deal in share trading and their derivatives. Whichever method you use to learn about investing keep this thought in mind and hopefully you will learn how to differentiate between the two major types of investments.

This book has been written purely as a standard form of investment strategy for people new to investing and savings. Whilst there are numerous investment types out there my focus on writing this particular book is to help you

> **Investments come in four basic types and they are property, equities or shares, government bonds and cash.**

understand that everyone can do this and we can all live debt free if we apply the simple principles in this book. By the way, if you know of anyone who is struggling financially you might want to pass this book on when you have finished with it or maybe even buy them a copy too. Sharing knowledge is powerful stuff and helping each other better understand how to get out of debt and control our own financial lives is what we should all be doing... now back to the book.

Investments come in four basic types. They are property, equities or shares, government bonds and cash. All other investments are derivatives of one of these four categories. Each of the four categories have their own unique investment criteria. If you want to invest in any of the categories be sure and learn the individual nuances of each. In particular the jargon or language used in each investment category which is different and can at times be confusing. Be sure to learn the relevant jargon as it will make the investment process a lot easier if you are speaking the right language. You might want to Google a dictionary of investment terminology as a possible starting point just to get your feet wet, so to speak. This will also help if you have a basic understanding of the language of investments when you speak with professionals like financial planners, and bankers and lenders and stock brokers etc. Given the diverse language used it will be time well spent. The first category of investment we will look at is property mainly because we all have a basic understanding of property given that we all need to live in a dwelling of some description.

Property investing is probably the most well known of the investment types. We can all relate to property as we all need somewhere to live, our businesses need premises to operate from and our government services need premises to operate from. Traditionally, property is seen as a medium to long term investment type although there are many strategies that you can employ to invest in property in short term lots.

As a medium to long term investment property it is usually held for its capital growth over the investment term rather than a short term income producing investment. Capital growth means that you would buy a property today for $x and sell it in the future for $x plus dollars. The increase on the value of the property we call a capital gain. Your capital, which is the property you purchased with money you invested has gone up in value and as such has created a capital gain. The true financial capital gain is the increase in your properties value compared to your purchase cost. Let's say you bought a property for $100,000.00, including all associated transaction costs, and paid $10,000.00 for the deposit. If in one year your property was re-valued at say $106,000.00 your property's value would have grown by $6,000.00. This equates to a gain in value of 6% over the year, or as we would say 6% per annum. This is calculated by subtracting the purchase price of $100,000.00 away from the new valuation price of $106,000.00, which is $6,000.00, and then dividing this amount by the original purchase price of $100,000.00 and expressing the answer as a percentage.

However, there is an interesting phenomenon at play here. Remember you invested only $10,000.00 of your savings into this property to start with. Well if we look at the return on your investment funds we see that you have not made 6% per annum as the property value shows, you have in fact made 60% on your money! Why? Because the gain of $6,000.00 when measured as a percentage of your initial investment of $10,000.00 is 60%! Wow! We call this the power of leveraging your money, but more on that later, for now we will continue our initial understanding of investment principles and get you started.

If you wish to invest in property you need to do lots of research and seek advice from licensed real estate agents or realtors as they are known in other parts of the world. Professional real estate agents can provide you a wealth of knowledge and can give you good guidance in regards to property in their local area. I need to stress here that real estate agents tend to be specialists in property values in THEIR local market. It is not unusual for an experienced real estate agent to be as lost as any of us if they are looking to buy property in a foreign market, i.e. a market other than the one they work in every day. It is their local knowledge that provides them with a competitive advantage over other real estate agents and as such when you go shopping for property look for an experienced agent working in their OWN LOCAL TERRITORY.

Buying property, or any investment for that matter when you do not have enough information about the investment type is fraught with danger and the best way to mitigate that danger is to KNOW your market before you buy. Research, research, and then research some more. You cannot do enough research when you want to invest. The more knowledge you have regarding your investment the better decision you are likely to make. Things like location, schools, public transport, environmental issues and other lifestyle choices are all things you need to research when buying property. Not to mention the costs associated with property investing.

> 

**The more knowledge you have regarding your investment the better decision you are likely to make.**

One of the key things you will learn about property investing is that the cost of doing business is high compared to other investment options. Property investing has many parts to it and some of the costs associated in Australia would be conveyancing, government stamp duties, building inspection fees, pest inspection fees, mortgage loan application fees, mortgage loan insurance fees, building insurance fees and solicitor search fees. These associated fees and costs add thousands of dollars to the cost of investing and as such property tends to be an investment choice once you have amassed a suitable amount of investment capital. Investing in property without sufficient capital is fraught with danger, so be aware. Investing

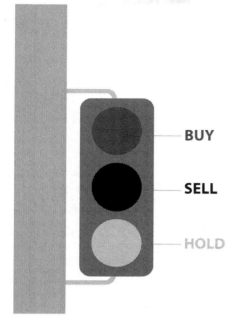

**BUY**

**SELL**

HOLD

in property in different states and countries has its own set of additional costs so be aware that it is not all the same. Different places have different rules, taxes and laws, so keep your advisers local. Deal with advisers who deal in the market you are looking at investing in. Many people have been caught out by ruthless marketers selling over priced property in markets that the individuals have no knowledge of. Stick to your own market and you will reduce this risk.

Investing in equities or shares as they are more commonly know is a lot less expensive and can be done with much smaller amounts of investment capital. The cost of transacting in shares is a lot less expensive and more easily identified as opposed to the costs associated in investing in property. Usually there is just a broker's fee for the purchase of the shares and this is a small percentage of the investment amount or it can be a fixed fee. There are many services advertised on the internet for share purchasing and most, if not all, will advise their fee up front to you. Like property investing shares too can be viewed as a long term investment but they are more liquid than property and as a result they tend to be more readily used as short term investments as well as long term investments.

Being more liquid means that they can be sold more easily in the open market and more quickly than a property can be sold. Selling shares can take minutes

> **As with property investing you can also leverage your share investments by borrowing money to invest.**

and money can change hands in a matter of hours or days, whereas selling property can take weeks or even months and money changes hands slowly, in fact in most property cases it is one month or more before the deals are finalised.

One other major factor in favour of share investing is that if you need to redeem some of your investment, but don't need to get all your investment money back, selling a small portion of your share investment would make this possible whereas as property investment tends tend to be sell all or sell nothing. You can't sell just the kitchen in a property sale or just the living room in your property to get money back, but you can sell fewer shares than you own. We call this *liquidity* and it is a key issue in short term investing.

There are numerous share types and this can be very confusing for a new investor, so as with all things investment, seek guidance and help from professionals in the field. Stock Brokers or Share Brokers as they are sometimes called will be able to give you sound advice as to what types of shares to buy and how to go about it. These people are specialists in the share market and can also provide you with study material which will help you learn the business of share investing. Many stock broking houses also provide seminars and courses designed to educate people in share dealing and are worth participating in if share investing appeals to you.

As with property investing you can also leverage your share investments by borrowing money to invest. In the share investment business these loans are called margin loans as opposed to mortgages in the real estate market. A margin loan is simply a loan provided by a lender to a borrower for the purpose of purchasing a parcel of shares in a lender approved company. Many lenders provide margin loans. Those who do have a list of approved securities, or shares, that they will lend against using the shares themselves as security for the loan. This is much like a lender lending money on a mortgage against a suitably approved property. Leveraging is also sometimes known as gearing, which simply implies that the investor has used some borrowed funds with which to invest, he or she is said to have geared, or leveraged their investment.

Investing in government bonds is similar to investing in shares but even simpler. Governments issue bonds to raise funds for capital works. These bonds or loans if you like are offered at a pre-set interest rate and are guaranteed to be paid by the government that is looking to borrow the money. You buy government bonds through a stock broker and they are usually for a set period of time, i.e. 5 years or ten years. At the end of the bond period the bonds are repaid by the government or rolled over for a further period of time at a new interest rate.

> Any money not earning interest
> is actually losing its buying power
> as time goes by.

Clearly it can be seen that these types of investments tend to be for the short to medium term and are regarded as being very secure, that is the interest payment and your capital is usually government guaranteed. Government bonds can be bought with nominal amounts of capital form as little as $1,000.00. It should be noted here that government bonds are regarded as the most secure type of investment available in the marketplace.

The final investment type is the type that most people start their investment portfolio with and that is cash. Cash investments are simply money placed on deposit in your bank or with a financial institution that earns interest. Money hidden in the garden or under the bed in a box is not investment and as such has the opposite effect for you. Because we live in a society that operates in an inflationary manner, meaning that things get more expensive as time passes.

**When you start your investment life you will, as mentioned earlier begin with a basic bank savings account.**

This also means that any money not earning interest is actually losing its buying power as time goes by.

Let's say that you consider buying a new fridge today and it will cost $1,000.00. You have saved the money and you are ready to buy the fridge. If inflation is running at 5% per annum the fridge, in one year, will cost 5% more, it will cost $1,050.00. If you had put your $1,000.00 under the bed and in one year went to buy the fridge you would be short $50.00 so you could not buy the fridge. Your money has lost some of its buying power. If on the other hand you put your money in an investment and it earned say 7% after one year, you would have $1,070.00 dollars in your investment account. You now go to buy the fridge, at the new price of $1,050.00 and you pay this amount, but voila you still have $20.00 left in your account. Your money has increased its buying power it has been working for you.

What does all this mean, well it means that instead of buying things with credit which commits you to working longer, remember the real cost of credit is the time you have to work to pay off the debt, you can buy goods for cash. By saving your money and investing you would have been able to buy the fridge in our example and still have $20.00 left in the bank. If your hourly earnings rate was $13.15 as mentioned earlier you would have in fact reduced your need to do future work by a little more than one and a half hours. That's one and a half hours of your future life you have just given back to yourself and your family. How good is that! A new fridge and some of your future life back in your "I'm not working life account" instead of your "I'm still working life account".

When you start your investment life you will, as mentioned earlier begin with a basic bank savings account. You will commit to putting 10%, as a minimum, of all your net income into this account each and every pay day. The bank account you choose at this stage should be a simple account with no bank fees and should pay you interest. There are many bank accounts out there that will do this so keep shopping until you find one that will meet your needs. Once you have amassed enough to broaden your investments you might consider investing in government bonds. This will lock your money away for a longer period of time and will usually pay you a higher rate of interest. In other words it will be working harder for you. Once you have decided to undertake more investing you will no doubt seek more specialist advice from a stock broker, real estate agent or licensed financial planner. Whichever option you take be sure you have looked at all the options and that the investment you choose meets your investment objectives.

Making your money multiply by working for you through you invested it will free you up from future labour commitments. Your future is yours to control and it starts with controlling your present. When you adopt these principles you will start to see a change in your financial affairs that will provide you with even more motivation and inspiration. Imagine your future where your money earns more each week than you can with your labour. We usually call this financial independence and many people take this as a sign that they can retire. Retirement with financial independence is what we all want, not retirement without financial independence. Your journey to financial independence relies a lot on how you put your money to work for you. You work hard for your money so be sure and have your money work equally as hard for you as you do for it.

So to recap thus far you have learned that paying yourself first is the best way to create wealth and that by then managing your money so that you stop the waste you will be able to live on less and save more. You have also learned that money can make money for you and the more you have working for you the more you will earn. Money working for you is a good thing. All good so far, and it gets better. In chapter four you will learn how to protect what you have from disaster and predators. Not predators who reside in the oceans but land-based predators who will want to take away your hard earned money because they can't make or save their own.

# PROTECT
# YOUR ASSETS

Once you have started to pay yourself first, controlled your spending and put your money to work you need to take appropriate steps to protect your assets as you amass them. It is not wise to work hard, put your money to work, buy assets and not protect them. Assets need protecting from all manner of things including theft by others, fire, damage and total loss due to catastrophe. You never know what lies around the corner and after all the work needed to amass wealth through asset accumulation you don't want to risk them. In fact the more assets you amass the more you should protect them because they will, in time, become your source of income. Once you retire from the workforce you will rely on your assets to provide your income for the lifestyle you choose to live.

Assets come in all shapes and sizes. Let's look at them and identify how to protect them. Firstly we will look at cash which is the basic unit of all investment and is the money you earn week in and week out. This money will usually be invested in the bank or similar financial institution and as such will be relatively safe. In Australia, we have very strong banks and government support for our banking system so your money is reasonably safe in the bank. When you invest in other institutions such as credit unions your money has less government support, the credit union will have less financial power than a major bank and as such your money is at slightly higher risk. This risk is usually demonstrated in the interest rate the institution will pay you on money deposited in your account. The higher the interest paid on an account, in fact on any form of investment, the higher the potential risk of loss of capital.

The next step in your investment will be to take some of your amassed savings and invest in some other form of investment. Probably it will be either some shares in a public company or a term deposit or a government bond. Of these investments the government bond will have the highest level of safety, followed by the bank term deposit with the share investments having the greatest risk of the three options. Government bonds are guaranteed by the government so there is very minimal risk of loss of capital with this type of investment. Term deposits in the bank are quite secure investments also. Shares on the other hand can be anything from minimal risk to very high risk and caution must be taken if you are investing in shares, even in the biggest of companies. Shares are open to abuse by unscrupulous investors who take control of public companies and destroy them. So be very careful when you invest in shares to make certain that you spread your risk across a number of different shares and that you also seek professional advice before buying. By investing in a diverse portfolio of shares you are in fact managing your risk which is an asset protection strategy that you should adopt.

The next asset class that we can all relate to is real estate or property and the first investment into property is usually for our own home. Clearly this investment needs to be protected and the easiest way to do this is with an insurance contract to insure the building against damage, fire and total loss. Insurance is relatively inexpensive and there are a large number of companies who will provide protection for you on your property. Additional protection of sorts is regular maintenance on the property. Property by nature deteriorates over time and therefore needs to be maintained, so a good maintenance program will keep your property in good order and this in turn will protect your investment from loss due to neglect. There are many properties out in the market that are poorly maintained and as a consequence have lower value than they would have if they were well maintained.

The final asset that you need to protect is probably the one most people neglect to protect or even give consideration to protecting. When asked what your most valuable asset is most people, especially home buyers/owners will answer their home is their most valuable asset and in some cases this will be correct. However, there is usually a larger asset than your home than MUST be protected at all costs. Any idea what it is? Imagine your home is worth $500,000.00, would you insure it. Of course you would. Now imagine that as a home owner your work at your job and you earn $50,000.00 per year before tax. Let's assume that you are 40 years of age and plan to work to retirement age of 65, that's 25 years of working. At an annual income of $50,000.00 per year for 25 years you will earn, without pay increases along the way, $1,250,000.00! That's more than double what you home is worth, but have you insured your income?

> **There is usually a larger asset than your home that MUST be protected at all costs.**

Another example is a person starting out on their wealth creation journey who has no real assets other than a stable job. Let's assume a person aged 20 earning $20,000.00 per year before tax. This person will work to age 65 so a total of 45 years of work and even without pay increases along the way they have an ability to earn a massive $900,000.00! This is their current asset value, their ability to earn this income. How much are you worth right now? The math is simple, take your current gross income, that is income before you pay tax and multiply it by the number of years between your present age and the age at which you think your will retire from work. The sums are astounding for us all and especially for the

high income earners amongst us. As you can see is it vitally important that you insure this asset.

Protection for this most valuable of assets is called income protection insurance and it is a must for everyone, as you can see from our example. Your ability to earn an income is quite possibly your biggest asset, even if you own a home.

Imagine if you are just starting out on the road to wealth creation, your income generating ability is probably the ONLY asset you have. So make sure you insure your income. It may not be possible for all of us to insure our income as insurers are very picky when it comes to income protection insurance and not everyone enjoys good health or has a job that is not too risky, say an abalone diver for example, a very dangerous job and practically uninsurable.

The ability to earn an income is the KEY to your wealth building activities without it there is little chance of you becoming financially independent. The good news for most of us is that we do have an ability to earn income and therefore we can adopt a wealth building strategy that will get us to our goal of being financially independent. Protecting your income provides security for the journey along the road to wealth creation. If you travel along the road without this protection you are placing at risk the one thing that you have that can secure your retirement future, your income generating capability. Without

**There is an old saying that says; "never put all your eggs into one basket", this saying applies specifically to investing your money.**

income coming in the only option you have is to live off your existing capital or savings which quite obviously will eventually run out. You need to keep adding to the savings account for it to grow. It is not designed for living off until such time as it can earn more than your living costs each and every month.

As you can see, protecting your assets is a key part of any wealth creation strategy but it does not end with insurance policies and choosing the right place to put your hard earned money. There are other dangers out there just waiting to separate you from your money. There are all kinds of scams and cons that will lure the unsuspecting investor and part them from their money. The internet is full of people trying to access your bank details to rob you, so be very careful how you handle your money and what transactions you perform on the internet. Keep your money in separate accounts to minimise the risk of anyone getting your bank account details and taking your money. By having your money in different accounts, even in different banks you reduce your exposure to risk and that is a good thing. One strategy I use is that when I make purchases on the internet I use a debit Visa card from an account that has a minimum amount of cash held in it. This way, if anyone gets those bank details the maximum amount I can lose is the cash I keep in that account. I make deposits into this account on an as needs basis. That is, I put money into the account when I know that I am going to make a purchase on the internet. This works for me, and may well work for you. Whatever you do, make sure that you protect your bank details form EVERYONE!

There is an old saying that says; "never put all your eggs into one basket", this saying applies specifically to investing your money. The wisest investment strategies have a diversification of risk which means the wise investor puts their money into a mix of investment types rather than putting all their money into one investment, i.e. putting all their eggs in one basket.

Spreading risk also provides an opportunity to create greater returns because investments run in cycles and at one time property may be a better investment than shares and yet at another time shares may be a better investment than property. Having investments in both gives you a spread of investments that should give you a higher averaged return and less vulnerability to the market. Whichever investment strategy you choose to use you should always protect your assets. Risk management through spreading risk is something that all prudent investors undertake so don't get caught up in investing in just one market. Even if you only like property as your chosen investment type, you can still diversify by buying different types of property in different markets. For example, you may buy a house in one location, an apartment in another location, perhaps some vacant land in another location or even some commercial or industrial property as well. By buying different types of property you are spreading your risk. Not all property markets move in the same upward or downward direction at the same time. Land may be scarce at any time and will increase in value whereas housing in another area may be in a downward motion due to oversupply. So keep your portfolio diverse and you will be managing your risk which in effect is protecting your assets.

One final component of major importance in asset protection is the management of the amount of gearing you use to buy assets. Remember, gearing is the amount of debt you have in relation to the value of your assets. Let's assume that you have bought a property for $100,000.00 and you borrowed $90,000.00 to make this purchase. Your gearing would be 90%. That is you borrowed 90% of the purchase price. Given that you have this loan you will incur interest costs associated with the loan. Interest rates can be set as fixed rates or variable rates and are open to changes. If you have a fixed rate of interest on your loan you only need to be concerned about interest rate movements when it gets close to the time when your interest on your loan is due for review. However, if, like most people you have a variable interest rate you need to closely monitor interest rate movements every month. You may find that your interest rate increases on a very regular basis, which in turn, will place a higher demand on available cash funds to make interest payments each month. It may be that these increases get so high you cannot afford to make repayments without suffering financial hardship. Beware, you do not want to find yourself not able to pay your mortgage due to increases in mortgage interest rate rises. If you find yourself in this situation you could lose your asset all together as the lender may exercise their rights under their mortgage and demand a sale of your property. Managing gearing is just like managing any other debt. You need to keep the repayments well within your means and also always have a safeguard against unexpected events occurring, like an unexpected repair bill or some other event that may affect your cash flow.

Asset protection, as you can see is an obvious thing to do. It is not wise to build up a very nice nest egg only to leave it vulnerable to the world at large. Protect your assets and they will protect you in the future.

To recap your learning this far, you have learned to save at least 10% of your income each and every pay day. You have learned that it is vitally important to manage your expenditure which in turn helps provide additional savings. You have also learned that you can and should put your money to work for you and that there are many ways in which you can do this. And in this chapter you have learned the value of protecting your assets, not just the ones you can see and hold, but also the non visible ones like your income and also protecting against gearing too highly. So now it's time to move onto the next chapter where I will teach you how to make your home a profitable investment.

> **It is not wise to build up a very nice nest egg only to leave it vulnerable to the world at large.**

# CHAPTER 5

# MAKE YOUR HOME A PROFITABLE INVESTMENT

One of the great Australian dreams is to own our own home and many people succeed. Whereas, once upon a time this was sufficient and our parents and grandparents were happy to achieve this in their working life it is not so today. In fact, whilst this was a challenge for many people in the past life was a lot simpler. Not so any more, the modern Australian, in fact most of the western world wants more. More assets, more money, more luxuries, more holidays, more education, better health, smarter kids etc, etc, etc. Is there ever enough for all the things we can desire in our lives, it appears not. With credit more abundant than in the past and a whole stack of mortgage types it is easier than ever to get into the home buying market. Not necessarily for the younger generation who are just starting out in their working life, but certainly for those people who have a few years work behind them and a good stable job. Buying your own home is achievable by many.

What happens then when you have got yourself into the home buying market and started paying off your mortgage, what then? Well, what you have done is given yourself a fantastic platform from which to launch your wealth building program. You have just accelerated your saving power and probably don't even realise it. Many people fail to understand the power of interest and taxation. You see, when you earn your money at work you pay tax on it and take home the balance. This we all understand. When you earn interest in your bank account and you declare this interest earned on your annual taxation return you pay tax on the interest, So far it is straight forward. Here's the twist, when you pay your mortgage you are in fact paying it with after tax dollars. When you invest after tax dollars in the bank as a savings account you are paying tax on the interest, so, what happens if you pay your mortgage with your savings instead of putting them in the bank. Answer, you do not have to pay tax on the interest because you do not earn interest on your home mortgage, you SAVE interest. Let's look at an example.

> **Many people fail to understand the power of interest and taxation.**

You have just bought your first home and your interest rate on your new mortgage is 7% per annum. This means in simple terms that for every $100.00 you owe on your mortgage you will pay the lender$7.00 per year in interest, so if you had a $300,000.00 mortgage at 7% per annum interest only payments your interest payments for the year would be $21,000.00, i.e. $300,000.00 x 7% = $21,000. Let's imagine that you are saving at a rate of $2,000.00 per year and your bank is paying you 5% interest on your savings, Your $2,000.00 in the first year would earn $100.00. You would declare this $100 in your tax return and pay tax thereon. If you are paying tax at say 30% your tax on your interest income of $100.00 would be $30.00. So, you would pay this $30.00 to the tax department and keep the balance of your money being $70.00 ($100.00 - $30.00). So in effect your $2,000.00 has

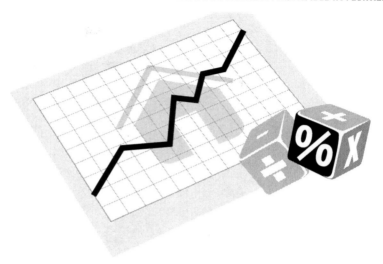

earned after tax $70.00 at the end of one year in the bank. Now consider what happens if you put your $2,000.00 into your mortgage account. Your mortgage charges you interest at a rate of 7% per annum, so, if you paid your $2,000.00 in to this account you would be saving interest on this amount at a rate of 7%. The answer is $2,000.00 x 7% = $140.00! You would have saved yourself $140.00 in interest payments to your mortgage. Added to this increase in earning there is also no tax to pay. Tax is paid on interest earned, not interest saved! The alternative, which was putting the $2,000.00 into the bank and paying tax on your interest earned, would have earned you $70.00. By paying the excess savings into your mortgage you are in fact better off by $70.00. You have doubled the return on your money through this one simple strategy.

As you can see from the previous example the advantages of home buying include the ability to accelerate the earning power of your savings. This is one of the greatest powers home buyers have over those who rent. Home owners have the ability to optimise their investment returns by investing in their own property. This investment also has a lot less risk attached to it as it is money invested into your own property, not at risk in a bank or other financial institution. But this is not the only advantage of buying your own home in fact this is probably the least advantage your home affords you. Through buying your own home a couple of other things happen over time.

**Owning your own home will give you more disposable income and as such a better investment future.**

Let's fast forward a few years and assume that you have paid off your home mortgage and now live debt free. You are in the same job and earning the same income that you were earning before. What has happened is that you now get to keep all your income for your living choices and investments. By not having a mortgage payment, or worse, a rent payment to make each and every month, you get to keep all that money to invest. Invest in what? Invest in your OWN future. How good would it be to get to keep all the money you earn each and every week? Well you can, but only through owning your own home. Owning your own home will give you more disposable income and as such a better investment future.

Benefits of homeownership are not limited to simply getting to keep your income it offers far more value than that. When you own your own home you own a very valuable asset. In fact you own just about the best type of asset you could own, especially from a bankers point of view. You see banks love to lend people money when they can secure their loan with a property. Borrowing money against the value of your home will allow you to invest those borrowed funds into other assets, such as property that will pay you rent and therefore increase your earning capability. Increasing your earning capability is after all the purpose of investing. You want to create as much passive income as possible for when you retire.

Passive income is income that you get without you having to work for it on an ongoing basis. It is passive income that will provide your lifestyle for you in your future years. Here you are not only putting your money to work for you but you can also put the banks money to work for you. Talk about accelerated earning power!

*"Hold on a minute!"* you say, *"How, can I own my home if I have borrowed money against it from the bank?"* Well the answer is you don't, anymore, what you have done is leveraged your asset, in this case your home, to borrow money to buy another asset. The new asset may not have any debt attached to it so you would own it outright and your home would have a debt on it. The key to remember here is that you have increased your assets by the amount of the debt, so if you sold the asset you could repay the debt and still own your own home. This can appear a little confusing and you would need to get some good advice on how to do this, but it is very common in wealth building strategies.

> Use your assets to make more assets and use leveraging to increase your asset base.

Use your assets to make more assets and use leveraging to increase your asset base. By leveraging your assets you will bring into play a number of taxation benefits that will also accelerate your wealth building program. It is important to note that the process of wealth creation is ever changing and as you amass assets that produce income or grow in value you accelerate your wealth creation activities, without doing more work. Consider the difference in real dollar earnings when we compare two investment amounts earning the same rate of return. Imagine investing $10,000.00 or $300,000.00 at 5% per annum return. The $10,000.00 would earn $500.00 whereas the $300,000.00 would earn $15,000.00. The same rate of return but very different dollar amounts.

Wealth creation accelerates as your assets get larger. So, if you can borrow money at one rate and invest it at a higher rate then you will make money. There are other benefits to accelerate your earning potential and one of them is taxation.

Taxation benefits for leveraged investments can be quite substantial and deliver a real boost to your wealth creation activities. Taxation deductions for things like interest payments, depreciation of assets, maintenance, and other costs

> **Interestingly, with wealth creation the closer you get to your destination the faster you get to move.**

can actually reduce the amount of personal income tax you pay. They reduce how much money the Tax Department takes out of your pay packet each week. This means you have more money to invest. The effect of this is one of accelerating your wealth creation by increasing your assets and reducing your personal tax payments. Ever heard of the old saying, "the rich get richer and the poor get poorer". Well these are some of the reasons why this is true.

You have to be *in the game* to *win the game* and with regard to investments and wealth creation it never gets harder, it gets easier as time goes by. Over time you save more money and get to invest in better assets, even to the point of buying your own home, then you get to leverage your home to get more assets and even better tax breaks.

The hardest part of the whole process is starting. There are millions of people out there today who want to get rich or create wealth but do nothing about it. It's too hard. What's too hard? Saving some money each week? Not wanting to pay yourself FIRST for all the work you do? Getting started is the hurdle you need to jump, and once over it the advice and help you need is in abundance for you to tap into. Starting every journey means that you are, at that point in time, the furthest away from your destination than you are ever going to be. The same with wealth creation; the start is the furthest point from where you want to be, you have the least amount of wealth. But, as with any journey, every single step in the right direction takes you closer to your destination. As it is with wealth creation, once you have started saving you are moving forward toward your destination or objective.

Interestingly, with wealth creation the closer you get to your destination the faster you get to move. You see, the more you have to invest the more you earn and the more you earn the faster you travel to your financial destination. Whereas, when we go on a walking journey we tend to slow down a little as we get further and further into our journey due to fatigue, or tiredness setting in. The sooner you start your journey the sooner you will reach your chosen destination, your objective of financial independence.

To recap your learning thus far, you have learned to save at least 10% of your income each and every pay day. You have learned that it is vitally important to manage your expenditure which in turn helps provide additional savings. You have also learned that you can and should put your money to work for you and that there are many ways in which you can do this. And in this chapter you have learned the value of protecting your assets, not just the ones you can see and hold, but the non visible ones like your income and protecting against gearing too highly. In this chapter you learned the value of making your home a profitable investment and that the sooner you start the journey to wealth the faster you will get there. So now it's time to move onto the next chapter where I will teach you how to create a future income.

# 6

# CREATE A FUTURE INCOME

As you get older you will inevitably lose your ability to provide your labour as a means to earn an income and you will need to utilise your investments to provide the income you need to maintain your standard of living. If you do not have investments that can provide the income you need you will be reliant on the aged pension which is not designed to provide for many luxuries. It is even less effective if you happen to still be in the property rent cycle. At least if you own your own home you have a decent chance of surviving on the aged pension. So the only real answer to having the money you want in retirement is to have an investment portfolio that provides income.

Calculating your required income is a subjective thing, especially when we are trying to project our needs into the more distant future. How much income will you need in your retirement? The answer can be calculated by looking at your current life style, is it what you imagine you would like to be doing in your retirement years? Are you doing the things now that you will want to do in the future? If so, then take heed from the figures that follow, for every $1,000.00 you spend today you will need a multiple of that in future years.

Let's imagine that the current cost of living is rising by 5% each year, or if you like we can say inflation is at 5% per annum. To buy in 25 years what you can buy today for $1,000.00 will cost you $1,437.00. Therefore if your life style today costs $40,000.00 per year to maintain then you will need 40 x $1,437.00 in 25 years which is $57,480.00. Now let's assume that the only way you can get this income, because you have stopped working is to have a lump sum of money invested to earn interest that will pay you $57,480.00 each year. Not allowing for any negative effect by taxation.

If your money is invested at 5% per annum interest then you would need a lump sum of $1,149,600.00! If this amount was invested at 5% per annum it would give you an income of $57,480.00 each year.

It is clear to see from the example that you really do need to create an income stream for when you retire and whilst building a lump sum of money like $1,149,600.00 seems nearly impossible to do, we do have, in our example, 25 years to do it.

So what do we do to get to this point of being able to fund our retirement lifestyle? Or, is there another way of creating an ongoing income in retirement without having such a huge amount of cash saved? The answer is yes, there are many ways you can create an income in retirement that will do the same as if you had $1,149,600.00 in cash. In fact there are so many ways that I could write another book just about that subject. For now though let's look at one of the key components of creating this income and letting time work in our favour.

One of the Australian public's favourite pastimes is property investing. There are tens of thousands of Australians who invest in property all over the country each year. Some invest in multiple properties whilst others are happy to just own their home. Many start out with very little in the way of equity but do have the other primary ingredients for property investing success. The initial ingredients you will need to invest in property are a stable income, a good credit rating, a sound investment objective and a deposit. Now, it is not uncommon for people to borrow the entire purchase price to invest in property because lenders see property investing as being very lucrative for them and so will lend against real property willingly. Property investing is so common and so effective that you really do need to understand how it works to your advantage. One of the key benefits of buying an investment property is it has taxation benefits that can reduce the amount of personal income tax that you pay, thus using money you would have given the tax man to provide for your own retirement. Now that is a good thing.

> **Property investing is so common and so effective that you really do need to understand how it works to your advantage.**

Taxation benefits of property investing, at the time of writing this book, include a tax deduction for property depreciation, land tax, rates, maintenance, insurance costs and interest charges on any loan you have to buy the property. All of these deductions can help put real cash into your pocket and not into the pocket of the federal treasurer. Seeking good financial advice is crucial before entering into any investment deal, especially a property deal, so do your home work and consult a professional when the time is right for you to invest. In the interim we will continue looking at how investing in a property will benefit you.

Imagine that you are able to buy a small investment property that is paying you $200.00 per week today and that you borrowed the money on a mortgage over 25 years. This means that in 25 years you would have paid the mortgage off if you keep up all your payments. Now, we will also assume that today you need to pay an extra $30.00 per week towards the cost of the mortgage after your tax benefits. The simple question would be can you afford to pay the $30.00 per week now. Answer, most likely yes. If so, what will happen over time is that the rent will increase as the cost of living goes up, your mortgage loan will reduce as you make payments and in 25 years you will have no debt and a regular income from the rent. The object of our exercise is to create income for retirement, remember?

> Your mortgage loan will reduce as you make payments and in 25 years you will have no debt and a regular income from the rent.

Assuming that our rental income went up by 5% per annum over the 25 years used in our example the rent in 25 years would be approximately $677.00 per week! Remember we wanted an income in retirement of $57,480.00 each year, which is $1,105 per week. Well, as you can see this little property deal could yield $677.00 dollars of that desired income. You would be more than half way towards your goal! How good is that?

Clearly, this simple exercise demonstrates that there are ways that you can start investing today, provided you seek advice from experts in the field of investing. What is most important though is that you need to create income to provide for your impending retirement years and the sooner you start the better your chances of providing a great income instead of a poor one. Without a quality, reliable income stream in your retirement years you will be living a life style that may not be all that you desire.

However, is one income stream sufficient? Should you rely solely on the investment property we just bought, or should you have multiple income streams? Multiple income streams are obviously a better choice and they are available too. You can invest some of your income into superannuation, or shares, or a business or an internet business. You might become an author or a musician or some other occupation that will pay you royalties for past works. There are lots and lots of ways to make extra income. Let's look at superannuation first.

Superannuation is a great thing for Australians in as much as the government provides taxation benefits for you for investing into your own superannuation fund. Much like property investing, there are benefits to be had that the tax man will provide for you. The tax man will do this to encourage you to provide for your own retirement, rather than have the country's welfare system support you through the aged pension scheme. One other special thing about superannuation in Australia is that it is compulsory for all employers to make contributions, or payments if you like, into the superannuation funds of their employees. That means that your boss has to put money into your superannuation fund for you every pay day. So in this regard you have a compulsory savings plan that is paid into by your employer. But what exactly is superannuation?

Superannuation is in effect a form of pension. When you reach your retirement age your superannuation manager will ask you how you want to be paid your superannuation benefits, and most people take a pension. In other words they agree for the superannuation fund manager to pay them a fixed amount of money each month for a set period of time. They receive a pension from their superannuation fund instead or in support of a pension from the government. This income is assessed against your eligibility to receive a government paid pension but with careful planning it may not all be assessed and a skilled financial planner will be able to best advise you on how to set up your superannuation benefits to optimise your taxation and pension entitlements.

As you can see superannuation can also provide a form of income stream available for you in your retirement years. I cannot stress enough how important this is, that you create income streams for your retirement years. It would be sad to say that after a life time of working for a living that you could not afford to keep

> **I cannot stress enough how important this is, that you create income streams for your retirement years.**

yourself in a lifestyle that you are comfortable with. You can buy property or businesses or shares, you can build a healthy superannuation fund for yourself and many more things, but the real thing you must do is put some effort into creating these income streams NOW!

Should you elect to buy a business from which you anticipate earning a regular income stream be certain and buy, or start a business that you can either sell for a big profit, and then invest the proceeds to produce the income you need, or start or buy a business that can be operated without your involvement. Should you elect to buy or start a business that you want to keep, but does not need your involvement, you may want to consider a franchise business. There are many franchises around today and many of them have experienced management structures in place.

There are franchises in Fast Food, Mechanical Repair, Retailing, Services and the list goes on and on. One of the best things about a franchise business is the support that is available from experienced operators if you choose wisely. But what exactly is a franchise? The answer is that a franchise is a business that you can invest into that has an existing operating system, product line, service and is fully operational. It is basically a business in a box. Small franchises can cost a few thousand dollars and have limited revenue opportunities whereas large franchises can cost hundreds of thousands of dollars to buy and can generate substantial income. Probably the most famous franchise in the market today would be McDonald's hamburgers. Many McDonald's stores are owned and operated by franchisees and as such these individuals operate a business using all of McDonald's technology and knowhow. The income generated from these franchises is split between McDonald's and the franchisee. Profitability can be very high, but as with all investment decisions you should seek professional advice if you are contemplating buying a franchise business. Owning and operating a business can provide income into retirement years.

> **A well planned and executed exit strategy will optimise your business return for you and give you a managed exit from the business.**

If you elect to start your own business it would be wise to seek professional guidance as to your exit strategy. This means that very early in your businesses life you should seek help, probably from an accountant or business broker as to exactly how you plan to exit the business. You will not want to find yourself at retirement age and having to try and sell your business, especially if the business economy is down, or flat.

A well planned and executed exit strategy will optimise your business return for you and give you a managed exit from the business. One of the key challenges of exiting a successful business is that many business buyers will want the owner of the business, you, to stay on for a period of time to affect a smooth changeover of ownership. This could be a number of years not just weeks or months. So plan well ahead and seek good advice.

Another very important aspect of selling a business is the taxation associated with the sale. You may find that you will have to pay some form of taxation on the sale of your business and this could have a negative impact on your overall profitability. Just as planning an exit strategy is important for any prospective sale likewise it is equally as important to plan the best possible sale which incurs the least amount of taxation liability. Your accountant will be able to provide you advice about the best way to minimise your potential taxation liability should you sell a business.

To recap your learning this far, you have learned to save at least 10% of your income each and every pay day. You have learned that it is vitally important to manage your expenditure which in turn helps provide additional savings. You have also learned that you can and should put your money to work for you and that there are many ways in which you can do this. You have also learned the value of protecting your assets, not just the ones you can see and hold, but the non visible ones like your income and protecting against gearing too highly. You learned the value of making your home a profitable investment and that the sooner you start the journey to wealth the faster you will get there and now you have learned how to create a future income. So, on we go to the next chapter, how to increase your ability to earn income.

# CHAPTER 7

# INCREASE YOUR ABILITY TO EARN

It seems obvious doesn't it that as you get older you should be able to earn more money per hour than when you were young. As you learn new skills and have more experience you should be able to charge more for your labour, and get it. Alas, this does not apply to many people, certainly not as many people as it could. It is not rocket science and improving skills and knowledge is open to us all. Are you improving your skills on a regular basis? Are you making a conscious effort to get better at what you do? How many books do you read each year? How many training courses do you attend each year? How much money do you invest in your own personal development each year? Your answers to these questions will be a true indicator of just how much value you are placing on your labour. If you want your boss to pay you more money, you need to demonstrate to your boss that you are worth more money. Perhaps it's not your boss who wants to pay you more money but someone else, a competitor of your bosses. Not to mention that the greater your skill level the more you get to pay YOURSELF!

It seems only logical that you would want to increase your earning capability as time goes by. Yet, so many people do little if any training or skills development after they leave school or finish their initial trade training. How can you expect to earn more money if you don't learn new skills? How can you expect to compete in the workforce if you don't embrace new technology, learn new skills and become more valuable to your employer? Living in the modern age we live in, where change occurs so rapidly it is imperative that you keep up to date with the latest skills set required to perform your job as a minimum. In fact, it is better if you learn new skill sets that you never had before. History is full of data about industries that no longer exist and as a consequence whole groups of people have lost their jobs as a result of new technology taking over.

My paternal grandfather lived through the late 1800's and early to mid 1900's in Liverpool in England. He was blessed with lots of height and strength. Measuring approximately 7 foot tall and being very strong he had two main careers when he started his working life. His first career was working on the docks in Liverpool as a labourer unloading ships as they came in. This was a very physical job and people were hired based on their ability to perform manual labour. His second job was a little more unique. When he was a young man the streets of his home town were lit at night with gas lamps and each and every night these gas lamps had to be lit by hand. Because he was so tall he could do the job more easily than most people because he didn't need a ladder to reach the lamps to light them. In fact, he was the lighting company's number one man because of his unique height. He had a job for life, for sure, until electric street lights were introduced. No one needs to light electric street lights so guess what happened to grandad. That's right, no more job! Had he not had other skills other than being so tall he would have been in deep trouble. This was not his doing, it was not his fault, it was progress and progress waits for no man apparently.

What is your current job like? Are you in an industry where technology and progress can eliminate your ability to earn a future income? If so, what are you doing about it? You don't need to just wait for progress to pass you over, in fact that would be the absolutely wrong thing to do. Go out and learn new skills, keep up to date with technology. Sound too hard? Maybe it is hard, maybe the thought of learning new skills is daunting for you as it is for many people, but here is the good news, we can all do it.

**Do you know that there is a direct correlation between the amount of books you read and the amount of wealth you acquire?**

I found a little secret that I would like to share with you about learning new skills and getting paid more for my labour. Do the things you really like doing. By doing the things you enjoy most you will be more motivated to do more and learn more. Just think of all the people you know who are successful in their careers and you will find they all love what they do. When you love what you do it is not like work it is more like fun, and when work is fun, it is fun to learn. Have you ever noticed that when we teach our children new things they learn fastest when it is fun and enjoyable? No one wants to learn when the learning is hard work. Adults are just big kids really so find a way to make your learning fun and enjoyable and watch what happens to you. You will acquire more knowledge and skills than you thought you could master when it is fun to do so. On the other hand, try and have someone learn something that is forced upon them and that is not pleasant and you will not get very good results. Why? Because learning needs to be fun and when it is we all want to do it.

Have you read any good books lately? Do you know that there is a direct correlation between the amount of books you read and the amount of wealth you acquire? I don't mean fantasy novels I mean fiction and books on specific topics. I do not know one single financial adviser or wealth creation professional who has not read dozens and dozens of books. Books are full of knowledge and knowledge is power and power equates to wealth. Not just financial wealth but physical wealth, spiritual wealth, social wealth, familial wealth, career wealth and emotional wealth. The great modern philosopher and teacher Dr. John F Demartini has read over 29,000 books! Imagine reading 29,000 books. Wow! That is amazing, but so is Dr. Demartini's breadth of knowledge. Knowledge

on a very diverse range of subjects and topics, but why does he do this? Because he is following his passion, a passion that drives him to be the best he can be, doing the things he loves to do the most. Can you read 29,000 books? Maybe or maybe not, but I bet you can at least read one book every couple of weeks. Even at one book every two weeks you will read 26 books a year and if those books are on a related topic before too long you would become an expert in that field. And we all know that experts get paid more than the rest of us, right? So, if you haven't read a book for a while or perhaps you read infrequently then you might want to start committing to more reading, because knowledge is power and power equates to more money.

Once you have picked up your reading activity you might want to consider reading a book about speed reading and learning this skill. Speed reading can be learned by most people and it will accelerate your learning, which in turn will accelerate your ability to make yourself more valuable to your boss. It is not a difficult thing to learn, it is more about practicing new skills than anything else. So go out and get a book on speed reading and experience the freedom reading quickly can give you. You don't need to spend days reading basic books when you can learn to read them in hours.

Another way to increase your ability to earn more income is to get fit. It is amazing just how unfit many people are today. So many people fail to look after their fitness levels. What does it mean to be unfit in the workplace? Unfit people do not have the energy to deliver as much productivity as fit people do, who are doing the same job. Productivity is one of the key drivers when employers assess employee value to the business. If you are the most productive person in your company then it stands to reason that your boss will pay you more than those people who are less productive in the same role. But there is more to fitness providing more productivity in the workplace.

> **People like to deal with people they know, it is that simple.**

The fitter you are the more energy you will have for other things in your life. Perhaps you can take up a hobby that may turn into a new career in the future. A friend of mine is into fitness as her hobby and as a result of her love of keeping fit she has now found herself doing a course on becoming a professional fitness instructor where she will, on graduating, be able to earn more money than she does in her present job. This is a classic example of learning new skill by doing things that are fun to the individual that deliver positive income results. So get fit and prosper. Fitness will also give you more energy to enjoy your life. No one wants to be tired and worn out all the time. Have you ever noticed that people who are fit tend to do more stuff than those less fit? It is clear from these few examples that one clear way to increase your wealth is to increase your ability to earn more money, even doing the same job!

What other ways are there to increase your ability to earn money? What about social networking? It is amazing how many people have very successful careers and earn lots and lots of money as a direct result of their social network. People like to deal with people they know, it is that simple. So, how many people do you know? How many people do you get to meet on a

> Not meeting any new people at all
> and in fact, not even keeping in touch
> with all the people you do know?
> Well now is your chance to change all of that.

regular basis? Perhaps you are not very socially active. You know, you get home from work each day and have dinner, watch a bit of television and then off to bed. Only to start over again the next day, and when the weekend comes around you do the basic household chores, play with the kids, have dinner, watch television and off to bed. Then on Sunday, more of the same with a view to getting ready for work on Monday. Not meeting any new people at all and in fact, not even keeping in touch with all the people you do know? Well now is your chance to change all of that.

Now is the time to go out and meet new people, do new things, explore new interests. Heck, even if you can't get to go out because of family restrictions you can still do all this on the internet. It is amazing how fast social network sites have blossomed. Facebook, You Tube, Twitter, Flickr and many more social network sites have sprung up all over the world and these sites are full of groups of people, just like you and me, sharing ideas and thoughts and interests, twenty four hours a day, seven days a week, it never stops. But how can these social networks help you make money and increase your wealth?

Social network sites on the internet are full of opportunities for people to learn new skills. There are forums you can join that discuss a multitude of topics. There are groups that meet on a regular basis to discuss and share their interests. There are sites that you can upload your pictures to and share with your family and friends in faraway places. In fact, there are so many things you can do you can create a whole new persona for yourself if you want to, all on line. The fact that all of these options are available means that you can now access more people in less time than ever before.

**Being part of a social network, or more than one, will improve your opportunities if you want it to.**

Got a new business idea you want an opinion of? Then post a message on twitter.com and tell thousands of people about it in one go. Want to know the answer to a question and don't know where to get it from? Ask the good folk on Twitter and see what happens. Someone somewhere will see your question and provide an answer for you. The more you use these amazing sites the faster your opportunities will grow. Why? Because social networks are about people finding out about people, they are about people sharing their lives and people helping other people. Being part of a social network, or more than one, will improve your opportunities if you want it to, but much like reading a book, you need to take some action to get started. It might look scary at first, but it really is very simple and a whole lot of fun. So do yourself a favour and enhance your income potential by joining in with the social networking system of the day. We all want to deal with people we know and trust and social networks allow us to get to know each other a little better, even if we live thousands of miles apart. By the way, social network membership sites are predominantly free to join, so what have you got to lose?

To recap your learning this far, you have learned to save at least 10% of your income each and every pay day. You have learned that it is vitally important to manage your expenditure which in turn helps provide additional savings. You have also learned that you can and should put your money to work for you and that there are many ways in which you can do this. You have also learned the value of protecting your assets, not just the ones you can see and hold, but the non visible ones like your income and protecting against gearing too highly. You learned the value of making your home a profitable investment and that the sooner you start the journey to wealth the faster you will get there. You have also learned how to create a future income. Now the learning has continued with your ability to increase your ability to earn more income either through education, learning new skills, becoming more productive and meeting new people to expand your network of contacts, all of which are designed to increase your wealth creation potential. Now it's on to the next stage which is where you will learn to manage your risk.

# CHAPTER 8

# MANAGE YOUR RISK

**Managing your risk is different from protecting your assets.** Protecting your assets is mostly about insurance and other methods to keep your assets safe; to protect them from catastrophe, theft, damage or loss. Managing your risk on the other hand is about managing the amount of risk you expose yourself too when you select assets to buy and the amount of gearing you use when you buy those assets. It is about keeping your assets safe from movements in interest rates, from sudden changes to your cash flow and from changes to your overall financial position. It is in fact one of the most important topics to learn when it comes to building wealth. Many people have amassed small and large fortunes only to lose them due to poor risk management. Even the best investments can go bad, so managing risk and controlling your exposure to risk is vital.

Risk management starts with understanding your risk profile. Everyone has their own risk profile and one of the easiest ways to determine yours is to consult with a qualified financial planner. In Australia it is an obligation of any licensed financial planner to, "know their client" and the key component of this knowledge is to know the client's, risk profile. Financial Planners do this with a simple questionnaire which has been designed to identify the client's aversion to risk. The reason this is so important is that ALL investment returns are based on a risk factor, the higher the risk, the higher the return on offer, the lower the risk, the lower the return on offer. There is a direct correlation between risk and reward and you need to understand this key aspect of investing.

There are a number of standard risk profiles and they are Conservative, Moderately Conservative, Moderate, Moderately Aggressive and Aggressive. Each of these five profiles identifies a different type of individual investor from a person who wants to accept very minimal risk, say a retiree who has limited income generating capacity and cannot afford to lose any of their capital, to a younger person who has a desire to get rich quickly and is prepared to gamble to some degree on their investment choices. Given that yields or returns are based primarily on risk you can see that to be conservative you will need to accept a lower rate of return on your investments than if you were an aggressive investor where you are happy to chase higher returns.

Whichever one you are it is important to understand that as you age and your circumstances change so too will your risk profile. What applies to you as a young person may well not apply to you as age.

Conservative investors tend to be intolerant of market fluctuations and as a consequence will usually be happy to forgo potentially higher returns in an attempt to avoid risk and see their hard earned investment monies decline, even if it is only for a short period of time. This would be typical of a retiree and once set in place their investments only need to keep maintaining momentum with inflation for them to be content. Investments utilised by conservative investors tend to be cash, government bonds and term deposits.

Moderately Conservative investors tend to be a little more tolerant of market fluctuations than their conservative counterparts, but they are still somewhat risk averse. They are usually accepting of minor downturns in their portfolio, but not long term losses provided they can get a little more return than the conservative investor. Typically investors who fit into this category are

## Moderate investors make up the vast majority of investment types.

either retired and getting their pay-check from their investments, or are people who are about to retire and are looking for a regular pay-check from their investments. Sometimes investors who have had a bad investment experience will fit into this category also. Both the conservative and moderately conservative risk profiles are what investment professionals would call defensive risk profiles. These people are looking for investment security above anything else.

Moderate investors make up the vast majority of investment types. It is these individuals desire to invest for long term, rather than short term gains that set the moderate investor apart. They are happy to accept some volatility in their portfolio provided they have an opportunity to increased gains when markets are rising. Investments that are rising higher than the market average in good times and falling lower than the market average in down times are the key objectives of a moderate investor. As a consequence of their balanced nature these investors tend to have a broader mix of investment types than say conservative or moderately conservative investors might and as such have more opportunity for gain, and also for losses.

Moderately Aggressive investors are the type of people who are daring and don't mind the see-saw ride of markets. Happy with some volatility provided they can occasionally get some big wins moderately aggressive investors tend to be younger and have more disposable income than their more risk adverse counterparts. These investors will have a tendency to use a higher level of gearing to optimise their investment returns and as such need to manage risk very closely to avoid serious losses. Being higher risk takers they will also tend to invest in new business opportunities and investment products more often than a risk adverse investor would. Moderately aggressive investors will tend to favour the share markets and will speculate on property investments where they think there will be short term capital gains, which after all, is what they mostly are seeking, not weekly income.

Aggressive investors are as the name suggests aggressive in their approach to investing. Aggressive investors will take more risk than all other types of investors and are looking for maximum gain. Usually short term investors by nature aggressive investors tend to favour the quick deals. They like to trade shares on a daily basis, or even quicker if it will turn a profit and are inclined to gamble more than most. Aggressive investors come in all shapes and sizes and are not usually categorised by age. They can have massive shifts in fortunes from one year to the next. One year they will be on top of the world and the next they can be down and out. Risk management is not their strongest point and as such they are prone to heavy losses if the markets move against them.

> Whatever type of investment profile fits you it is important that you understand what it is.

Whatever type of investment profile fits you it is important that you understand what it is. By knowing what your profile is you will give due consideration to investments that fit your profile. By investing in investments that suit your profile you are more likely to feel comfortable with your decisions. Whereas, if you invest in investments that are opposed to your basic profile you will no doubt feel somewhat uneasy and will want to end your investment as soon as possible.

It is not uncommon for conservative investors to feel great levels of stress if their investments are going poorly. Likewise, aggressive investors can become quite impatient if their investments are not performing as well as they would like them too. Whilst these are not necessarily bad occurrences, investors who have invested in the wrong asset type for their individual profile will oftentimes make rash, poorly assessed decisions about those investments and act out of angst rather than from an informed decision. Many times suffering unnecessary losses just to get out of an investment that they don't feel comfortable with.

If you find yourself making investments into areas that feel uncomfortable to you firstly ask yourself is it because the investment type is new to you, or is it going against your basic investment profile type. If it is a new type of investment and you have invested in line with your own personal risk profile then the more you learn about the type of investment that you have invested in the better you will feel about it. Whenever we do something new for the first time it is natural for many of us to feel a little apprehensive. If, however, you have made an investment decision that is contradictory to your personal risk profile then no matter what you do the feeling of discomfort will probably stay with you until such time as you liquidate the investment and invest in something with which you feel more comfortable.

So, as you can see risk profiles are an important part of making an investment decision and one you should pay close attention too. Equally important in risk management though is debt management.

Managing your debt is one of the most vital parts of risk management. Whenever you borrow money to invest it is crucial that you have a strategy for managing that debt. Understanding that interest rates move upwards and downwards and as a consequence the loan repayment amounts you are currently paying may well move, up or down and these movements may add to your available cash income or diminish it.

> **Equally important in risk management though is debt management.**

A very good rule of thumb to adopt when looking at your debt management is to make certain that your loan repayments are never more than 30% of your net income. That is, 30% of your take-home pay after tax. This should be a maximum debt ratio, not a minimum one. It is one of the biggest errors in wealth creation that people make, being too highly geared. It is great when things are all going along smoothly, but if there are negative changes to the economy and interest rates rise you could find yourself in hot water so to speak. People do not lose money on assets until they sell them for a loss. So if the market turns downward and you find on paper that your investment is worth less than before don't panic. You never incur a loss until you sell and if you do not need to sell all you need to do is wait for the investment to come good again, most often they do.

Another good habit to adopt in risk management is to make sure you always have at least 6 months living costs available to you in the form of readily accessible cash reserves. Much like rising interest rates can cause cash flows to get out of hand a loss of job could be catastrophic. Be sure to always have six months of living expenses in reserve, that way if you have an unexpected loss of income you will have time to handle your investments in an orderly manner until such time as you commence work again.

**Other strategies for risk management include corporate ownership of assets and the use of trusts.**

It is the unexpected that we are trying to protect against and this is mostly what risk management is all about. Life is not always rosy and investments run in up and down cycles, so be aware it will not always be going the way you planned, but a good risk management strategy will help you look after your investments.

Other strategies for risk management include corporate ownership of assets and the use of trusts. These are advanced risk management tools and should be used only with professional legal and accounting advice. Suffice it to say in this book that when you are well on your way to creating your wealth you will be introduced to these strategies by your financial planner and your accountant. In a nutshell these strategies involve the creation of either a trust or a corporate entity with which to purchase your assets. Whilst these two types of entity are different they both achieve one thing in common. They can protect your assets from creditors and if you are prone to being highly leveraged in your investment activities they are probably something you need to investigate. But I will repeat; they are to be used only with professional legal and accounting advice.

CHAPTER 9

# SET GOALS AND COMPLETE THEM

There is no doubt that one of the most powerful tools you will ever use in your wealth creation activities is the use of goals and effective goal setting. By setting goals you are in fact giving yourself the best possible chance of success. It matters very little how big your goals are, what matters is that you set them and that they are achievable. I will discuss in more detail later exactly how to set effective goals, but for now let's look at why you would set goals.

Imagine you are about to embark on an ocean cruise around the world. You have booked your cabin and you are all set for the vacation of a lifetime. Relaxing, while cruising the seas and being waited on hand and foot. Oh what luxury and how good are you going to feel! But wait there is a problem, the captain of your beautiful ocean liner has not made any plans. He hasn't organised the cruise so he has no idea which way he is supposed to head. He has no idea where he is supposed to be at any point in time, has no idea where he will refuel or pick up more supplies. In fact, without a plan your captain will probably not even leave the dock and your wonderful

>

**You just keep adding to it and measuring your results and you will see that the goal will become real.**

holiday will be spent sitting on your luxurious balcony overlooking the docks. What a disaster, or would you prefer he just sail off and see what happens?

Without setting goals and having a plan your ship's captain would be taking a huge risk going to sea without a detailed plan. He will plan exactly where he will be at the end of each day's cruising; he will know ahead of time when he will reach different ports to refuel and pick up supplies. He will have a method of checking his progress every hour of every day so he stays on course and if something unexpected happens along the way he will adjust his forward plans. Without all this detail he would not be assured of getting to his desired destination, of achieving his goal! Very much like you and me when we want to achieve something, if we don't have a plan we will most likely fail.

There is an old saying that people who fail to plan are simply planning to fail. This is so true.

If you have a goal and you write it down and follow through it will more than likely become your reality, it will manifest itself in your life. By having a detailed plan you will be able to determine at the outset if what you are striving for is doable, if you have the resources necessary to achieve your goal or if you need to collect some resources along the way. You will know beforehand where you should be at any point in time along the journey, helping keep you focussed and on track. A clearly defined goal is one of the most important steps in wealth creation. So let's look at the structure of goal setting.

When you embark on your goal setting activities it is good to start with the end in mind. What is it you want to achieve? Let's assume you want to save

$1,000.00 or any other amount of money for that matter, the principle is always the same. So, to start we look at our goal of saving $1,000.00 and we write that down at the top of a piece of paper. Next we decide by what date we want to have the $1,000.00 in our bank account. Let's say in one year's time. Next we break the amount down into smaller goals by time, i.e. If I want $1,000.00 in one year then what should I have in one month? The answer could be 1/12th of $1,000.00 or $83.33. So if I have saved $83.33 at the end of the first month then I am clearly on my way to having $1,000.00 in twelve months. In two months I should have 2/12ths of $1,000.00 or $166.66 saved and so on all the way up to 12/12ths, or $1,000.00.

From this simple exercise we can clearly see that we have an amount in mind, a goal of $1,000.00 in one year and we know that we should have $83.33 at the end of the first moth if we are to be on target. But what happens if you can't save $83.33 per month, what if that is too hard? What choices do you have? Does it mean that you can't save $1,000.00 in one year? Should you abandon your goal? The answer is simple. You don't abandon your goal you just modify it. You can modify it by either extending the time to suit your saving capabilities or you can find ways to earn more money so that you can save the desired

**The whole purpose of this exercise, to set realistic goals and achieve them.**

amount. Either way you will achieve your goal and that is the whole purpose of this exercise, to set realistic goals and achieve them.

Let's assume that you can only save $40.00 per month. If this is the case then you divide your goal amount of $1,000.00 by $40.00 which is 25 and then you know that your realistic time frame for saving $1,000.00 is 25 months. At the end of the first month you will have saved $40.00 and at the end of the second month you will have saved $80.00 and so on. You just keep adding to it and measuring your results and you will see that the goal will become real.

The key to success is to never give up, just keep going safe in the knowledge that if you keep going and you are on track then you KNOW you will succeed!

**It is impossible to amass a million dollars without amassing say the first $100.00 or $1,000.00.**

This is one of the most valuable lessons in creating wealth, knowing that what you are doing is taking you ever closer to your goal.

Having a written goal adds more energy to your endeavours. It is quite amazing the changes that come over us when we are winning. When things are going our way they tend to keep getting better, we get more inspired, we get luckier and people and events seem to come together to help us. Some say it is universal law and others call it god, but whatever it is it happens and the more effort you put in to planning your life the more things will come to you, it just does. It seems the richer you are the more money you get; the healthier you are the healthier you get; the more giving you are the more you have to give; the smarter you are the smarter you become and so on. In regards to wealth the more money you have, the more money you get.

Many people will say they want financial independence or to be a millionaire and yet they do nothing to head in the right direction. It is impossible to amass a million dollars without amassing say the first $100.00 or $1,000.00. Sure you may win the lottery or inherit a fortune from a long lost relative, but if you want to make a concerted effort to create your own wealth then you need to start at dollar 1 and go from there. The journey is taken one step at a time whatever your journey. You cannot go from England to Australia in one move, you must have stops and check points along the way and saving money is no different. Likewise you cannot go from $0.00 to $1,000,000.00 in one move, it takes time and commitment, but it can be done in pieces, one step at a time. The secret is to develop a plan and set goals that are realistic and then you have a better chance of success.

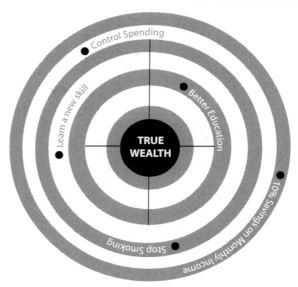

Goal setting is not just limited to the financial aspects of your life. Goals can be set for anything that you want to achieve be it getting a better education, learning a new skill, losing weight, stopping smoking and the list goes on. The magic is in the check points. The little targets we set for ourselves along the way. As I mentioned earlier there is a kind of magic that happens when you look at your goals and identify that you are on target. When you can look back and clearly see where you have come from and look forward to where you are heading. These moments of reflection seem to summon up the universal forces that control all of life and give us new drive, more energy and somehow change how we see things. A new image of ourselves, a new way of looking at what we are capable of. This is wealth creation on a holistic scale not just a financial scale. True wealth is not measured in money alone, but more in the quality of life you get to live.

Living a high quality life affords you opportunities of exploring your own capabilities and with these explorations new ideas, new ways of making money, new ways of helping people, new ways of being the best you can. Many highly successful people are not just financially rich they are rich in many other ways and that is what you can achieve. If money today is not in abundance in your life but you feel that you want to create wealth then start your goal setting in

**If you want to learn about money one of the best ways to do it is to do it in small bits.**

other areas of your life. It may be on education about money, like reading this book for example. Set up a plan of attack and go for it. In fact, one of the best things you can do whilst money is not in abundance is increase your knowledge about money. Libraries and the internet are free sources of knowledge about money and the more you learn about money the easier it will be for money to come to you. You will attract it more easily when you become more familiar with what it is and how it circulates.

As a starting point, identify how much time a day you can spend reading. Now you may be like a lot of people and say, "I don't have time to read" and like most people you would be wrong. We all have time to read we just need to identify what that means.

Let's imagine that we are going to sit down and read a novel. We would normally think that we need a few hours to sit and read to be able to enjoy the story and you would probably be right. However, if you want to learn about money one of the best ways to do it is to do it in small bits. Why? Because we want to learn and not just be entertained. When we read novels we are reading in a passive mode, we want to relax and be entertained. When we read to learn we need to read in a more focussed state so that we retain what we have read. The best way to do this it to ask yourself this question before you start reading, "why am I reading this and what do I want to get form it?" If you are reading a passage about interest rates then you might ask the question what are interest rates? Or how do interest rates affect income? And so on.

Once you identify the purpose of your reading the reading becomes more effective. Imagine if you could read one page of a book every day or one chapter even.

A 365 page book would take one year to complete at one page per day, at one chapter per day you would probably read two books per month! At two books per month within a short period of time you would be seen as knowledgeable about any subject that you put your attention to. How long will it take to read one chapter per day depends on your reading speed and your comprehension of what you are reading, but if you spend 1 hour per day reading, even if it is broken into 4, 15 minute sessions you will be amazed how much you can get through. Can you find 15 minutes in the day? Of course you can, everyone can if they really want to and especially if they have set it as a goal.

Effective goal setting is paramount to wealth creation whether it is setting savings goals or income goals, or learning goals. Whatever it is the more goals you set the more you will see yourself achieve and the more you achieve the more you will want to achieve, it creates a perpetual motion. Not setting goals leaves you wandering in the mist, not sure where you are going or how you are going to get there. Which would you rather do, travel the journey you set for yourself or wander around lost and reacting to whatever circumstance comes along?

# CHAPTER 10

# DO NOT SPEND RETURNS UNTIL THEY ARE MORE THAN YOUR NEEDS

Once your money has started growing and working for you, you may find that you will have a tendency to start spending it. **Don't!** Unless the income from your money's earning activity is more than enough to meet your lifestyle expenses and even then only if you have to. What we are trying to do in wealth creation is to provide a means of funding our chosen lifestyle without the need for US to work. That is to say we want our money to do all the work for us so we can sit back and relax. Until you get to this point, you need your money to keep growing and make more money for you.

Imagine you had a field and in that field you could plant a crop that could sustain you and your family forever provided you kept tending to the crop. This crop is never completely harvested; it is merely picked as your life's needs dictate. That way it keeps growing and getting bigger and bigger until one day you realise that you can even now support your extended family and friends. This magnificent crop just keeps on feeding you and your family with very little work. What a great crop to have. Or, you can plant your crop and when you see that it is ripe you pick it all and consume it. Then what? You might still own the field, but with no crop to grow, your field is not as valuable. You need to then go out and buy another crop to plant. This costs you money and the crop is new and not mature so it yields less than the older established crops. Which way do you want to grow your crops?

The smart investor will invest their money just like the first crop owner. They want their money to keep producing fruit so they leave it in the investment to generate maturity which, in turn, yields more fruit. Have a look at established plants and their crop yield compared to young plants and their crop yield. The more established plants will invariably generate higher crop yields than young plants.

Likewise money that is invested for longer periods and left to grow will yield greater returns than smaller amounts invested periodically. The longer you save the more you save; the richer you become. Wealth is built over time not in days or weeks but in years and generations. Have you started your wealth building for your future generations?

One of the best rules to use when deciding to spend some of your investment funds is to calculate if the balance of your investment funds will actually pay for all your living expenses and continue to grow. Let's imagine that you have an investment of $400,000.00 and it is earning 5% per annum in interest. We will ignore taxation matters for this simple exercise. Your earnings on your investment would be $20,000.00 per annum. Now, if your living expenses were $60,000.00 per annum quite clearly your investment income is not sufficient to pay your living expenses and continue to grow. So, don't touch it and keep adding to it to make it bigger. In fact in order to pay all your living expenses at an earning rate of 5% per annum your investment nest egg would need to be $1,200,000.00. That is, $1,200,000.00 earning at 5% per annum produces income of $60,000.00 - your living expense total per annum. However, we still need our investment fund to grow. If you take out your earnings each year from this point on your investment amount would stagnate. It would always be $1,200,000.00 because you keep taking the profit. What you want to happen is for it to keep growing so let's look at what you should do.

You need to keep adding to your investment account until such time that you can clearly see if you take out your living expenses that your investment will earn more next year than your budgeted living expenses. By making sure that your investment earns more than you spend you are assured of wealth because by constantly keeping and investing your surplus income you will get rich, it is just a matter of time. As I said wealth is created in years and generations not days and weeks.

> **As I said wealth is created in years and generations not days and weeks.**

This happens as a result of two events working in your favour. Firstly, if you keep saving the amount you have must go up. The second is more profound and it is called the compounding effect. This is the true magic of wealth creation so let's look at it.

Compounding means adding interest onto interest. Let's look at an example to see it more clearly. Imagine you have invested $1,000.00 into a fixed term account at 5% per annum for 10 years. Now, $1,000.00 times 5% equals $50.00. So we should earn $50.00 each year for ten years, that's $500.00 right? However, when we compound our interest something amazing happens. At the end of the first year we will have earned the same $50.00, no big deal here. At the end of the second year however we earn our $50.00 but we also earn an extra 5% on the first year's $50.00 profit that we made which is another $2.50 so we will have at the end of our second year our initial $1,000.00 plus our first years income of $50.00 plus our second years income of $50.00 PLUS our compounding interest of $2.50 for a total of $1,102.50.00. We would be at this stage $2.50 richer than just getting a flat 5% each year on our money. Doesn't sound like much but at the end of ten years this would be $1,628.89. On our flat earning rate we would have had $1,500.00 so we

> By being patient you will allow
> your investment to catch up with your lifestyle
> and that is what you are striving for.

are ahead by a whopping $128.89! If we invested for twenty years our flat rate account would have $2,000.00 in it whereas our compounding account would have $2,653.29! What about 30 years? Try $2,500.00 compared to $4,321.93! And 40 years, $4,000.00 compared to $7,039.96 - a whole $3,000.00 more! As you can see compounding interest is a very powerful tool and if you continue to add regular savings to your investment the effect is even more powerful.

The key issue here is to learn patience so that your investment has a chance to grow and compounding can become your friend. By being patient you will allow your investment to catch up with your lifestyle and that is what you are striving for.

You want to be earning more than you are spending with a surplus that remains invested.

This is true financial independence but one trap that awaits many potentially financially independent people is the rise in living costs. For many people as they amass money they tend to raise their lifestyle expenses. They drive better cars, they dine out more often, they move to a better neighbourhood, they send their kids to private schools and the list goes on and on.

This is a real challenge for many and one of the best ways to deal with it is to increase your lifestyle expenses in line with your investment earning capacity before the change and after the change. What you would do is look at your investment earnings compared to your current lifestyle choices and see if there is a surplus. Then, look at your investment earnings compared to your lifestyle choices after the proposed change in lifestyle. If the investment income after the proposed changes still yields a surplus then you could go ahead and make the changes. If, on the other hand the investment income does not cover all

**By sticking to your plan and working on your goals you have a better chance of achieving financial success than if you don't stick to your plan.**

your proposed lifestyle change expenses then you should re consider making the change at that time. This is where the patience comes into play.

By being patient and adjusting your lifestyle to meet your financial capabilities you give yourself the best possible chance of success in reaching your goal of financial independence. We call this living within our means. Living within our means however does not just mean not getting into debt, it means living within the boundaries we set for ourselves in relation to our income and the things we have decided to do with that income. The key component of this is to pay you first, remember? It is sad to say but inevitably when people choose to change their lifestyle the first thing to go is the regular saving plan they have adopted. They stop paying themselves first and use that money to fund other lifestyle choices. By sticking to your plan and working on your goals you have a better chance of achieving financial success than if you don't stick to your plan. Remember, people don't plan to fail they fail to plan and all good plans require a degree of patience to come to fruition.

One other important aspect of not spending you returns until they are greater than your needs is that the greater your investment returns become the broader your horizons become. Instead of hoping to buy a new Toyota motor car you raise your expectations to wanting a new BMW or Mercedes Benz or Porsche. You will raise your expectations about where to holiday and where to live, where to educate your children and what to wear, where to dine and a million other things that life will offer up to you. By taking time and acting prudently you can have a greater choice of things to do and buy than you will have if you act hastily. The farmer who pulls out his crop before it is ripe loses money compared to the farmer who harvests his crop at the right time and replants for the next season. As I mentioned earlier, wealth is a long term proposition not a get rich quick process and the longer you work at it the richer you get. The richer you become the more you can do for yourself and others and the more you will find to do.

View your investments like a crop. Tend to it regularly, keep it safe from the elements as best you can, nurture it and only take that what you need and let the rest just keep on growing and before you know it you will have acres and acres of crops to choose from. You will be able to feed yourself and your family for years to come. It is from small acorns that large oak trees grow.

# SEEK ADVICE ONLY FROM EXPERTS IN THEIR FIELD

Imagine you are driving down the road on a beautiful sunny day and all of a sudden you here a clunk in the engine bay of your car. Your heart sinks and you think "Oh no, not a break down, I can't afford to be broken down". But alas, your thoughts are right and you have broken down. Now what? So off you go to the doctors and you say, "Doctor my car has broken down and I know you like cars because I've seen you at car auctions and things and we have talked about cars every time I have come to see you, so could you please come and fix my car?" And the doctor, being a car fan and wanting to help says to you, "No problem, happy to help. You know I love tinkering with cars, they are my hobby and I will do what I can to save you some money and help you get your car back on the road." So off you go and the good doctor fixes your car.

A few days later you hear an even bigger clunk and sure enough you have broken down again. So off you trot to your mate the doctor and say, "Doc, I've broken down again and I think it is the same thing, but it was a fair bit noisier this time than last time, what do you think?" "Well," says the doctor, "I wasn't a hundred percent sure when I fixed it last time that it would work ok, but it started and you seemed to be doing ok, I'll have another go for you." Only this time the doctor can't fix it. In fact the problem is so bad that you need a new engine. "What happened you ask the doctor? "I don't know." the doctor replies, "But it sure is broken now." The net result is you now have to go to a mechanic and get your car fixed properly by a true professional. The cost, who knows, but it would have been much better had you gone to the mechanic in the first place.

The story you just read may sound a little contrite and too simple for belief but this sort of thing happens on a regular basis. It might not be your doctor who "knows" about cars, it might be your brother or your best mate, your neighbour or a friend of a friend, but one thing for sure, unless it is a mechanic it is risky and when it comes to your investments it's very risky.

Taking advice from anyone other than an expert in the field is fraught with danger and you cannot afford to gamble with your financial future by trusting it to amateurs. History is littered with well intentioned friends and family that have caused severe financial loss. You've heard the stories of the person who trusted their family member or friend with some great investment advice only to lose the lot. It sounded like a great idea and the friend or family member's passion for the idea was infectious, but alas, taking advice form an inexperienced person is dangerous.

Are all professionals good at giving advice? Not necessarily, like all things in life, some advisors are more experienced and have more skill than others. It's all relative to what you want advice on. The best way to determine if the advice you are getting is good or not is to ask you advisor if they are doing what they are advising you to do and how has it worked out for them. If the advisor has no firsthand experience in the type of investment they are recommending then how on earth can they give proper advice? Now I can hear some financial advisors saying that is not true, that they don't need to do the same thing to understand the consequences of the action they are advising you to take. You don't need to put your hand into boiling water to know that it will hurt and that is correct, but if you have ever put your hand into boiling water and got burned I am sure you would have a greater respect for the degree of pain it might cause.

**I ask for advice from those who walk the walk, not just talk the talk so to speak.**

When it comes to investment advice my rule is to seek advice from professionals in THAT particular industry. If I want advice on property investing I will seek it from a specialist who invests their own money in property. If I want advice on shares I will seek it from an advisor who invests their own money in the same type of share I am considering and so on. I ask for advice from those who walk the walk, not just talk the talk so to speak. There is only so much knowledge one can glean from reading books and going to school. Real knowledge comes from doing and in investing this is the key. So which practicing investment advisor should you look for? Well there are two types.

The first type is the one who can clearly demonstrate their success in the investment that you are looking at investing in. If it is property then look for successful property investors in your area and seek their council. One good way to do this is to start with a real estate agent or realtor as some people call them and ask them who the most successful person is that they know in real estate in your local area. Then approach the person you identified and ask them for their advice. It is amazing how freely many people will share their knowledge with someone with similar interests. You can do this many times and talk to many successful investors.

The second type of advisor you want to track down is the one who lost money in the investment you are looking at. These may be a little more difficult to find, but they will be able to tell you why they failed and until you fail you may not be aware of the real dangers you are facing. Ask your family and friends if they know of anyone who invested in the investment you are considering and can they introduce them to you. Once you get the opportunity of talking to them ask them what happened and don't forget to ask them who they got advice from. Was it their doctor?

Why is this so important? Why is getting advice from both sides of the coin so important? The answer is that you need to make informed decisions about where to invest your money. By doing this you are less likely to act in haste or on emotion and will more than likely make better choices. Better choices can mean less risk or at least a better understanding of the risk you are taking. When it comes to money and investing there are many people that can tell you what to do with your money, yet they don't do it with their own. Why is that do you think?

Getting advice about what to wear to dinner or which movie to see won't have a huge impact on your life. Advice on these sorts of matters we can take from just about anyone; if they were wrong the consequences if any, are usually minimal. If the movie was not very good; so what? You wasted a few dollars and learned something about the person who told you to go see it; but when it is about your financial future you need to get

> Professional advice is worth its weight in gold.

professional advice ONLY. It is odd that people will offer advice freely to you about what to do with your money, as freely as they might recommend a movie but the consequences of taking their advice could be catastrophic. It is amazing how many friends or family members are experts because they read a book about investing or saw a TV show all about property investing or went to a seminar one day to learn all about it.

Professional advice is worth its weight in gold. When you seek advice pay for the best advice you can get form the best source you can find. It will pay you dividends it the long term. Imagine you are in your mid 40's and have a family with young children at school, you have a mortgage, a steady job and a few dollars saved and you are thinking about investing for the future. You have a choice of two advisors who have been introduced to you. Advisor number one is a mid twenties aged financial advisor who graduated from college a few

**The issue is it's your money and when it comes to investing your money experience should be your yard stick.**

months ago. They are single, living at home with their parents and are very keen to help you. They are very professional in their demeanour and are very friendly towards you. The second financial advisor is a more mature person aged in their late 50's who has been in the financial advisory industry for 25 years, has raised three children, paid off their own home mortgage and is investing for their own financial retirement. Which one do you want to give you advice?

Let's look at the two alternatives. The first adviser is very keen to demonstrate their knowledge. They have just graduated so would be up to date with all the latest investment strategies and economic theory. They are very likeable and happy to provide good service. They are limited in their life experiences when compared to your own and those of the other potential advisor. They have no children to raise and no mortgage to pay so they probably would have some difficulty in relating to your real life issues. Whereas the second advisor has been there and done what you are going through, they have raised a family, paid off a mortgage and are even working on a real plan for their financial future. They appear on the surface to be succeeding in their endeavours. They can relate to exactly what it is you are trying to achieve and with the tools you have available to succeed. So which one do you choose? Advisor Two clearly has more experience, especially in your circumstances than Advisor One so I would suggest in this instance you go with the experience, especially if they are successful. Now this is not to say that advisor Number One could not do the job, not at all. In fact they may even be better at it than advisor Number Two. The issue is it's your money and when it comes to investing your money experience should be your yard stick. There is no substitute for actual real life experience!

**XY FINANCIAL PLANNERS**
1532 Business Square  Midwest 3209
Phone: (02) 8839 5100

Name _____

Address _____

# R

- Eliminate credit card debt
- Invest in stocks

An experienced professional will be able to give you insights into wealth creation that you may never have realised even existed. Their practical knowledge may save you lots of heart ache and even accelerate your success, so be sure and seek it out. When people have invested their own money and risked their own future in their decision and have been successful then they deserve our attention and we should listen to what they have to say. Rhetoric is one thing but cold hard cash is another and when you consider how hard you have to work to get your cash then you might want to work just as hard at getting the right advice. These people are out there and they are willing to help if you ask, but just remember this, you don't go to the butcher if you have a toothache, you go to the dentist!

# CONCLUSION

# PUTTING IT ALL TOGETHER

So here you are having read the 11 steps that you can follow to go from being a basic wage earner to having financial independence. So what do you do next? The answer is simple start today by paying yourself first. It is never too late to start creating your own financial independence, the sooner you start the sooner you will get to where you want to be. Is it too late for you? Feel like you're too old? Think again. Even at age 60+ it is not too late to start. Why? Because the average person in the western world will live into their eighties! That's 20 plus years of living past age 60. How do you want to live those years? With or without money! One of the greatest challenges people find in wealth creation is starting the process. Excuse after excuse is given as reasons for why we can't do it. The reality is that all you need to do is follow the 11 steps in this book and you will create a better financial world for yourself than you have today. Neither age nor financial situation should deter you from starting on your journey to financial independence, today!

Following these 11 steps will lead you to your financial goals. Will you achieve them? Who knows? It all depends on what your goals are. Are they realistic, are they achievable and are you committed to succeeding? These are all part of the process. Simply following the 11 steps will get you there but it does need input from you. It is not enough that you have read this book, or any other book on wealth creation for that matter. Books can only provide you with information about how to do something they cannot do it for you, only you can make things happen. Making things happen is what life is all about. It is a fantastic journey to be part of, not to merely be an onlooker. Likewise, financial independence is there for the taking, provided you partake in making it happen for you.

Some of the steps in this book may seem to be daunting or at best require a shift in your thinking. A wise man once said that the definition of stupidity is doing the same thing over and over again, but expecting a different result. Clearly, if you do the same things again and again then you will inevitably get the same results. But if you want the result to be different, i.e. you want to be more financially independent, then you must change the things you are doing that are not working towards making you financially independent. These 11 steps are proven to work for anyone who follows them. Perhaps they are new to you, or you may have even heard about them before but never acted on them. Here now is your chance to change the way you do things around money. Here

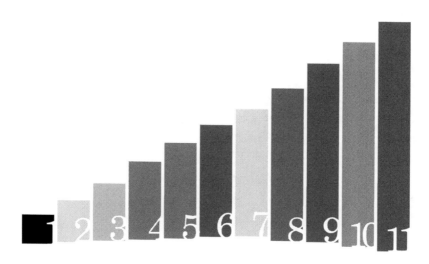

**With a little love and care and attention you will find money does grow on trees.**

is your opportunity to do it right and get to where you want to be financially.

One of the great challenges to people who have little money is to accept that in order to save one thousand dollars you must first of all save one dollar, then another dollar and so on. It is not difficult to save one thousand dollars provided you stay focussed on doing just that. It doesn't matter how long it takes you, what matters is that you do it. For some people it will be relatively easy to save their first one thousand dollars because they earn a lot of money. For those less fortunate to earn a high income it is just a slower process that's all. Don't let the time it might take you stop you from starting. Like plants that grow in the ground. We plant them as seeds and nurture them until they are fully mature. In some instances this can take several years. It may even be that the plants don't yield any fruit until they are mature, but once they produce fruit they continue to do so provided you look after them properly. Saving and making money simply requires the same process.

Congratulations on getting this far. You are now equipped to change your financial circumstances forever. So go on, plant your own money tree today by starting to pay yourself 10% of everything you earn as a minimum. Follow the other 10 steps and before you know it you will have a money tree that will provide you with years of pleasure and financial freedom. With a little love and care and attention you will find money does grow on trees.

# ABOUT THE AUTHOR
## DAVID H NOLAN

As a graduate of Monash University with a Degree in Business, majoring in Marketing, David has spent his career in a range of industries all related to wealth creation. Starting his financial career in Finance with a multinational money lender he moved into the challenging area of Life Insurance Sales. Progressing over time into the field of Financial Planning where he not only operated as a licensed Financial Advisor with his own client base he also taught other Financial Advisers a broad range of financial management skills and systems.

David believes that anyone can create financial independence irrespective of basic education levels, current financial position and physical capabilities. The processes are there for everyone to learn and to put into practice. There are no excuses, only lack of belief and action.

Made in the USA
Charleston, SC
28 May 2016